The Financial Healer

Mark Bristow

DEDICATION

To everyone who, in their own small way,
is trying to make the world a better place.

CHANGE YOUR SELF-WORTH,

INCREASE YOUR NET WORTH.

CONTENTS

Mark Bristow

1 THE SONG REMAINS THE SAME

The rain came down even harder onto Alex's car as he sat idly drumming his fingers on the steering wheel. Not that the rain was slowing down his journey in any way, the traffic was nose to tail for as far as he could see.

"One hour and 15 minutes to travel six miles; not so long ago I could run it faster than that." By now, it was 7.30pm. "Rush-hour?" Alex thought to himself, "That's a joke, more like rush three hours."

Alex had been in a bad mood for most of the day. He had started out with such good intentions; he had got into the office early, consulted his "to do" list and had actually started work on the first item. However, he had then been distracted, helping his colleagues with their technical queries, making coffees for everyone, taking phone calls from other people's clients because nobody else would, and so by lunchtime he had not completed item one.

His day went steadily downhill in the afternoon when the monthly sales figures were published. Optimistically, Alex looked at the top of the list before moving down the page; once again, he found himself in the bottom third, the equivalent of five out of ten at school; must try harder. "Why does this always happen?" he thought to himself, "I have more knowledge than most of my colleagues. I am well liked and generally get on well with my clients. I always put the hours in and I'm willing to help anybody. The advice I give to my clients is at

1

least as good as anyone else's and I always act with honesty and integrity, so why am I still in this situation?"

The situation that Alex found himself in was that, at the age of 41, he was divorced, living alone in a rented property with credit card bills and loans totalling £35,000. This, despite spending 25 years working in financial services!

Alex wasn't totally unhappy. He was popular both in and out of work and had many friends. A workmate had described him as "one of the good guys", which comforted him a little during those times when he was beating himself up inside for not being as good as his financially successful colleagues.

He was generous, he would always be first at the bar to get his round in, and always contributed the most to any office collection. He played a number of sports and was always seen as a team player. In his twenties, he had volunteered for a local hospital radio station, which combined his love of helping people and music. Alex had often thought that, in the words of Bryan Adams in 'The Summer of 69', "those were the best days of my life".

In school, Alex always did OK. An aptitude for figure work pushed him towards a career in Life Assurance; well, that and the fact that the interview was easy (a school friend had told him that). The company had great sports' facilities, free lunches and his mother had stated that it was a job for life!

Alex had a great relationship with his family, spending a lot of time with his mother after his father, whom he idolised, had died when Alex was 34. Recently, his mother had met someone new and whilst he was not Dad, he was a good man and treated Mum well.

Alex's sister, Suzanne, was the quiet one of the family. She would tell you that was because she could never get a word in. Like many marriages, hers had its ups and downs, but Alex liked her husband Tom (they had played for the same football team and often socialised together). Suzanne and Tom had two daughters whom Alex spoilt in the absence of having any children of his own.

Getting a girlfriend was never a problem for Alex; however, sustaining a relationship that lasted more than a couple of years was. It seemed like he was always looking for that "perfect" person who would tick all of his boxes. As a result, these relationships at best fizzled out and at worse caused a lot of heartache for his ex-partners; something that he was not particularly proud of, and for which he felt particularly guilty.

The light, indicating that the car was short of fuel, lit up and Alex was immediately brought back to his financial situation. He was reminded of his mother's expression "cobbler's shoes". The word "cobbler" dates back to the middle ages and describes those who spend their day mending shoes. However, the cobbler's own shoes were often in a state of disrepair with his toes hanging out of the front. When Alex thought about his finances, this particular metaphor had more than a hint of realism. He chuckled to himself when he remembered that he had even spent a year of his life living in Northampton, the home of the cobbler!

Another one of his mum's sayings was "Don't do what I do, do what I tell you" – wasn't that the truth!

It was a further half hour before Alex made it through his front door, via a local fast-food outlet as by now he was feeling far too tired to even contemplate cooking for himself. He sat down and ate his TV dinner which tasted good for five minutes and about which he felt guilty for the rest of the evening. He then went over and opened his briefcase and took out his "to do" list for that day. Despite getting to the office at 7 o'clock, well before most of the other staff arrived, and before the phone calls from clients started, Alex only actually managed to tick off three items from his list of ten that he had to do that day. OK Alex, concentrate and do some work now and tomorrow will be different.

He didn't, and it wasn't.

In fact, it was the same the day after, and the day after that, which subsequently turned into weeks and then months.

In fact, very little had changed. A year on and all that seemed to happen was that Alex was becoming more and more frustrated by the day. The pattern would always be the same. Alex would get up early so that he got into the office and avoided interruptions. However, he would never get done what he set out to do and so he would bring work home in order to "catch up". The work stayed in his briefcase whilst he fell asleep on the sofa, only to wake up and watch mindless TV until the early hours of the next morning.

It was during one of those TV-watching sessions that he came across an "infomercial" from a self-help guru. You are probably aware of the type of thing – basically a commercial with a cheesy American voiceover that takes twenty minutes to try to sell you something, when probably it could all be done and dusted in a minute. Well, this one promised to change every aspect of Alex's life. That was good enough for him and he was sold on the idea.

For the next few weeks, Alex listened intently to the guru and was impressed by his enthusiasm and considered a lot of what he said made sense. It certainly helped the often long journeys to see clients seem much less arduous and it was a welcome change from the familiar tunes coming out of the radio. Indeed, there were days when he felt incredibly positive and, for a while, believed that things were finally changing for the better.

Before he knew it, however, most of the positive thinking had fallen away and had been replaced by his old habits. He found himself in the same old routine – wondering why it was that he wasn't as successful in all areas of his life as those around him. In particular, he wondered why he never followed his own advice regarding finances and was actually in debt at a time of his life when he should have been looking forward to being financially free.

The more he thought about it, the more frustrated he got. After all, he was a financial adviser and there were no excuses. His parents had been good with money and had encouraged him to save; he had no addictions to feed (except perhaps a slight overspend on concert tickets and CDs) and could not even blame the constant drain on money known more commonly as children.

Alex knew what he had to do yet he consistently didn't do it. He had put himself in the position where money was controlling his outlook on life and was sapping his energy. If anything, his financial situation got worse as he would buy himself clothes and CDs that he didn't really need, that provided instant gratification, but nothing else other than further stress when the credit card bills arrived.

One day, whilst looking for his car insurance certificate, Alex came across a book he had first read some ten years previously entitled *The Magic Of Thinking Big,* which essentially stated that the way to get on in life is to put a positive slant on everything, and, not surprisingly, to think big. He sat down and read the book again and began to feel better.

"Everything would be better in a year's time," he thought. "When I have received my bonus payment, I will pay off the credit cards and loans, and start saving."

Things didn't get better, and he didn't start saving.

During that year, Alex struck up a friendship with a much younger girl. At one time, it looked as if it might develop into a more serious relationship. Whilst this boosted his ego for a while, it seemed to him that this was the beginning of a mid-life crisis. In reality, a fully blown mid-life crisis was never likely as he didn't like motorbikes and his slowly developing bald patch meant that re-cultivating his 1980's mullet was never going to happen. So the thought of a mid-life crisis brought the end to the friendship; that and the fact that she decided to go out with someone her own age!

Work wise, things were actually improving slightly as he implemented some of the guru's techniques which he managed to remember for more than a few weeks. As a result, his bonuses increased. However, the more he earned, the more he spent, with the net result being that his financial situation remained the same.

"Is there an expression that doesn't involve a swearword to describe aptly just how frustrated I feel at this moment?" Alex thought to himself. "Maybe frustration to the power of ten? That just about covers it. Things aren't as bad as they were for the self-help guru: I'm not living out of the car and having to hold down three jobs just to survive, so why do I always make it so difficult for myself?"

Although he was grateful that he had not suffered such hardship, somehow, this made everything seem even more frustrating. Every night, he would source the Internet, looking for that one guru with the magic wand that could wipe out his financial worries at a stroke, that one bit of advice that would put him on the road to riches. He also read books and listened to CDs in his car that promised the secrets to ultimate wealth and to live happily ever after. Whilst the books and discs gave lots of techniques and invaluable information, ultimately nothing much changed.

Alex began to wonder whether he would ever be in control of his finances. Although he did not know it yet, the man who was to ultimately provide the answers was soon to enter his life.

As he began to wonder whether he would ever be in control of his finances. He recollected a quotation he had once heard:

"If you always do what you have always done,
you will always get what you have always got."

2 GOING TO CALIFORNIA

I t looked like another frustrating day when Alex pulled up outside the office. One of the advantages of getting to work early was that he didn't have to spend up to thirty minutes looking for a parking space, which would have been the case had he arrived at the same time as the rest of the workforce. As he searched his pockets for the office keys, he looked up and noticed that the office lights were already on. This was somewhat surprising and slightly annoying for Alex as he liked to be the first in the office; even if only so that everyone else knew it, and that somehow gave him some sort of credibility. What was even more surprising was that the person who had made it into the office before him was Richard, the director of the Financial Services Division.

Richard was very much from the old school and had run the division for fifteen years. Before that, he had made his money in the "good old days" when commissions were high and not questioned and legislation was virtually non-existent. You would go out in the morning and spend an hour with a client arranging a mortgage before returning to the office to write a confirmation letter and send the forms to the relevant organisations. At worst you may have had to telephone a couple of clients and then the rest of the day was your own.

With his good looks, impeccable dress sense and his public-school accent, Richard had been successful in his work and private life and was now reaping the benefits of his sales force. With the help of a couple of very experienced administrators and a fantastic marketing strategy that continued to produce new clients, the advisory department basically ran itself. He spent most of the day being wined and dined by sales representatives desperate for a slice of the ever-increasing cake that the company was generating.

"Morning Richard," Alex said. "Is there a big sales meeting that I have forgotten about?" A sales meeting was normally the only time that Richard made it into the office before 9.30.

"No, nothing like that." Richard replied, "I got an e-mail from Harry and it just says 'whatever', and I don't really understand it."

"What? Just one e-mail that says 'whatever'?"

"No, obviously there's more to it than that. You know that he had gone off to California to learn about that Neuro Lingual thing."

"You mean Neuro Linguistic Programming, NLP."

"Yes, that is it. Well, he said that whilst he was out there, he met someone called the Financial Healer who has changed his life and he is not coming back to work here. Obviously, I e-mailed back and said that he had to work his notice period and that an explanation for his actions would be welcome. That is when he replied with the 'whatever' e-mail. I don't understand, why would he throw away everything he has here?"

"Yes," thought Alex, "why would he throw away everything?" Harry had been the top sales person by a country mile for a number of years now. He often earned in a month what Alex made in a year and had a big house, a great looking wife, big cars and his children at a private school to prove it. As top salesman, Harry was given the best introductions and the best administrative support. It seems that he had everything in place to make his working life as easy and as lucrative as possible, so why was he leaving?

It was another three weeks before Harry returned to the office, and then only briefly to clear his desk. He was a brute of a man and had played rugby and boxed professionally before embarking on a career in financial services. Alex and his colleagues had often pondered whether some of his clients actually felt intimidated by him. Certainly, when he wasn't happy, he was someone to be avoided.

This was a different Harry though. He was smiling, seemed to be pleased to see everyone and moreover seemed at peace with the world. Gone was the aggressive "sell, sell, sell" attitude that he inevitably brought with him to the office; Alex had likened Harry to a rough version of Gordon Gekko from the film *Wall Street*. He even said on occasions that lunch was "for wimps".

Alex was pleased to see Harry and relieved at the same time that he appeared to be in the best mood of his life. Even though he was not keen on the hard-sell attitude, he actually respected Harry for his positive outlook and his work ethic, and, in return, Harry liked Alex because he put in the hours and was always willing to help on technical issues. Ever since he had heard that Harry was leaving, he had wanted to see him, just to ask him why. Why give up his position of earning twice as much as the next top adviser with all the administration support and clients that everyone else craved?

Although the other advisers thought that with similar support and access to clients that Harry had, they would be as successful as him. It was not true.

"Hi Harry, sorry to hear that you are leaving. I know you are busy clearing your things but I have to ask, why? Why are you doing it? You work hard, you've earned the right to have the pick of the clients and with the admin support you have, it is easy street now. I just don't understand it."

Harry looked down at Alex, smiled the broadest smile Alex had ever seen and said:

"You need to see the Financial Healer."

"What? The Financial Healer? Is that who you travelled 2,000 miles to see? The Financial Healer? Why would you need a financial healer? You are earning nearly as much as the rest of us put together."

Harry repeated, "You need to see the Financial Healer."

That was as much as Alex got from Harry that day. Despite repeatedly asking him for at least a bit more information, Harry just kept smiling and told him that he needed to see the Financial Healer.

It certainly was a different Harry that came into the office that day. Richard, who appeared sometimes to be trapped in some sort of time warp, had concluded that he had taken too many drugs whilst in California and the Financial Healer was head of some hippy commune, while the rest of the sales force were contemplating which of Harry's clients they might be offered.

It was a different journey home that night. Instead of beating himself up over what he had not done that day, Alex reflected on the change in Harry. Instead of this person who, at best, epitomised controlled aggression, there had been an air of calmness, the like of which Alex had never seen before. Gone was the extreme competitive nature, replaced by someone who seemed totally at ease with himself.

Alex made a decision there and then: he needed to see the Financial Healer.

Alex's excitement soon turned to dismay as the next Financial Healer course was in three weeks and there was no way he could get all of his work up to date and raise the money for the trip. For the next thirty minutes, he drew up a list of reasons why he didn't need the Financial Healer and then looked through his e-mails and various "guru" websites to find the magical answer to all of his problems. Finally, he opened the e-mail called "Weekly Words of Wisdom" and came across something that seemed as though it was written for him, right then and there. The words read:

"How much longer are you going to make excuses? How much

longer are you going to ignore what is right before your eyes? How much longer are you going to live a life of frustration?"

Although he tried to ignore it and erase it from his memory, he couldn't get those words out of his mind. He kept visualising Harry and remembering just how contented with life he seemed.

It was time to take action.

It is a funny quirk of the financial system, certainly in the UK, that the more debt you have, the more the credit card companies are willing to let you have, and therefore Alex had little trouble getting his credit limit increased in order for him to pay for the trip to California. Having enough holiday entitlement was not a problem as Alex had always planned his holidays for when his work was up to date – it never was.

As he hit the "pay now" button, Alex felt a wave of relief come over him. Despite the additional expense, he felt that this was a positive step forward. He read the confirmation e-mail and then noted that there was pre-course work to complete.

First of all, he was to list all of his assets and liabilities. This was a little painful in terms of the end result. The exercise itself was easy to complete as this was what he did with clients every day. When he looked at the end result, though, it made for painful reading.

Secondly, Alex was asked to work out a rough estimate of what he had earned during his working life. "That's an interesting one," he thought. "I have never even considered what that figure would be."

Finally, Alex was to write down everything he spent in the following week. Nothing, but nothing, was to be left out. Everything had to be listed. He had actually attempted to do this before, with the idea of finding out where all of his money went, but he had only kept it up for a couple of days. This time, he would see it through. After all, he thought to himself, what was the point of flying halfway round the world, using up all of your holiday entitlement, and going further into debt if you were not going to put in the work.

It is amazing how much work can be done if there is a big enough goal at the end of it. Alex was determined to go to California without the worry of what was left behind on his desk. So for the next three weeks, he kept his head down, delegated what he could, and was not the first to offer help to his colleagues. Instead, he politely told them that he was too busy and he had things to complete before he went away. As far as his work colleagues were concerned, Harry had gone mad and therefore Alex was not going to let on that he too was going to meet the Financial Healer. Instead, he told them that he had met a girl online, called Mandy, who lived in Pittsburgh and that he was off to meet her in person. Rather a little white lie than three weeks of mickey taking!

As he boarded the plane to Los Angeles, Alex's prominent emotion was that of relief rather than that of achievement. Anything he hadn't managed to do wasn't particularly important and he had contacted his clients to say that there would be a delay in getting some information to them. Within him, there was a nagging feeling that if he only worked all the time as he had for the previous three weeks, then life would be so much easier.

Once he was on the plane, Alex started to relax. Once you are on board, there are not a lot of other things to do. No one can contact you, and you can't contact anyone. After burning the midnight oil for the previous three weeks, he actually began to look forward to the next two weeks, hoping that they would be life-changing.

It was with a mixture of trepidation and excitement that Alex entered the seminar room. During his working life, he had been to many seminars but these were nearly always work related. The majority of the time was taken up with dry presentations outlining recent changes in legislation so that the relevant boxes could be ticked to say that he had completed enough hours of "continuing professional development".

This time, it was going to be different.

3 NOBODY'S FAULT BUT MINE

Despite dealing with the public all the time, Alex was slightly backward in coming forward when it came to mingling with strangers and chose instead to take a seat quietly on his own. Looking around, he was pleasantly surprised to see what he considered to be normal people. After the initial positive feelings around taking the first steps towards changing his life had subsided, he had experienced a few doubts: would the course actually be any good? Had he wasted yet more money? How stupid will he feel when he has to admit to the rest of the delegates that he was a financial advisor? Would the course be full of hippies and had Harry actually been brainwashed?

"So," thought Alex to himself, "the delegates look normal enough; in fact, some of them actually look quite affluent judging by how they are dressed. I wonder what they are doing here? "

Overriding everything, however, was the intrigue of the Financial Healer. Alex had failed to get any more information about him from Harry and the website gave little away – other than that his mission in life was to help people overcome the barriers that stop them from enjoying abundance in their lives. Rather than some hard-sell sales letter, the website was very soft in its approach and did not appear to be the sort of thing that would appeal to Harry at all, which just served to make it even more intriguing.

At the front of the room there was a casually dressed guy who was quietly testing the equipment. "He must be one of his helpers," thought Alex, when, at that moment, the guy clipped a microphone to his shirt and said:

"Hi everyone, I am Jakap, the Financial Healer; thank you for being so punctual. Please take your seats, we are about to start."

Alex was somewhat taken aback. The Financial Healer had been shrouded in a certain amount of secrecy; there seemed to be no pictures of him on the Internet and certainly not on his website. "Well that is a surprise," said the man who had sat down beside Alex. "I was expecting at least someone mystical, dressed in a robe and with a visible aura," he laughed. "Hi, I am Dan, by the way, I work in financial services, good to meet you."

Alex was beginning to feel at last that he had come to the right place.

The Financial Healer spoke again and thanked everyone for coming. He appeared to be genuinely pleased to see everyone and, as Alex looked around, the room seemed to have something that he had never really experienced in a seminar or course before. That feeling was one of positive energy. "I hope this guy is good," he thought to himself, "because the expectation levels are incredibly high."

The positive energy seemed to disappear instantaneously as Jakap announced, "OK, instead of the usual thing that happens at seminars where you turn to the person next to you and introduce yourself, I want each of you to take it turns to stand up and introduce yourself. "

Immediately, Alex started to feel nervous. Generally, he did not mind getting up and speaking in public, provided he had some notice, was able to prepare and knew his audience. He had read somewhere that according to one particular survey, over half of the population would rather die than speak in public. Alex usually took those surveys with a pinch of salt; after all, he had never met anyone who had taken part in one of those surveys. However, judging by the look on some of the faces of the other delegates, this particular survey did not appear to be far off the mark.

"Only joking," continued Jakap, "but just take a minute to note how you felt when I made that suggestion as that will become very important later on. In reality, you will have plenty of opportunities to get to know each other over the next few days, and a lot better than you might think.

"Now you are really worried!" he laughed.

"I know that a number of you have travelled great distances to be here in order that you can have a better relationship with money and discover how to obtain abundance. Well, I have some bad news, this course isn't going to do that, oh no …

"This course is going to change your lives!"

"Boy, this guy really has to be good," Dan whispered to Alex, "because he has just sent the expectation levels in here through the roof!"

Jakap went on to outline some ground rules to the course: "Now first things first, I don't have all the answers, but I have attended a lot of courses, asked a lot of questions, read a lot of books and have a passion for changing lives. What I will teach you is based on my own view of the world, my learning and my own experiences. So let's start with some basics:

"Money is important …

"Regardless of what some people may tell you, the above statement is true. If you don't think that money is important, speak to somebody who has none.

"However, in my opinion, money is not the MOST important thing. The richest man I know, currently worth over $2 billion, is not happy. He is obviously a very successful businessman and has the number one company in his particular field, but happy? No. He has no real interests outside of work and believes that his wife only married him for his money. Even work doesn't really interest him anymore now he has achieved his goal of being number one.

"Money does not buy happiness …

"Money alone won't buy happiness, despite what advertisers may have you believe. As well as those that have more money than they will ever need but are not truly happy, there are many folk who have very little money and are very happy indeed.

"At the very least …

"Money buys financial security, which in itself may help towards an easier lifestyle. It is fairly well reported that one in three marriages ends in divorce and that the biggest contributing factor to these divorces are financial problems. Whether the marriages would have survived if the financial problems were not there is up for debate, but it is probably true to assume that at least some of them would.

"At best …

"Money can buy you freedom. Here are some of my favourite quotations on this subject:

'Wealth is not about having a lot of money; it's about having a lot of options.'
Chris Rock

'Money is only a tool. It will take you wherever you wish, but it will not replace you as the driver.'
Ayn Rand, *Atlas Shrugged*

"So as you all know by now: I am the Financial Healer, so let's get healing.

"First of all, we need to find the extent of the problem and that is why I asked you to come prepared with your list of assets and liabilities. So, who is going to be brave and tell me their net worth?"

Dan raised his hand and said, "$150,000, give or take a few cents."

"OK, that is great, now how much equity do you have in your home?" Jakap replied.

"Oh, about $200,000."

"So, if we take out your home, your main residence, the figure is actually a debt of $50,000?"

"That is about the long and the short of it."

"OK, thanks Dan for being the one who breaks the ice and being the first one to share with us all.

"Here is my take on this …

"You might think that your greatest asset is your main residence and in some countries home ownership is actively encouraged, but is it really that much of an asset? On an ongoing basis, unless you are renting out one or more of the rooms, it is actually more likely to be a financial liability. There are utility bills to pay, you will have the cost of repairs, as well as insurance costs and mortgage payments.

"You will only create an asset when you sell and only then if you downsize to a less expensive property."

The Financial Healer continued, "Oh, and for those of you that have listed your cars as assets, unless you own a classic one, those nice-looking bits of metal on your drive or in your garage are a constant drain on your finances as you pay for petrol, tax, insurance and repairs. Of course you could sell your car and maybe make a few dollars, but you would then have the inconvenience and cost of public transport."

Jakap then asked if anyone else was willing to share his or her net asset figure and rather to Alex's surprise, a number did.

Unsurprisingly, the figures were not good, with the highest being a positive $25,000.

"Well, if you aren't feeling great right now, guys, I am afraid it is going to get worse before it gets better, for a short time anyway. For the next exercise, what I want you to do is to go back to your pre-course work and look for the figure that you have calculated as being the total amount you have earned since you started working."

Alex stared blankly at the piece of paper in front of him stating £425,000. As he was in the USA, he had also written $640,000, the rough equivalent.

$640,000 earned and all he had to show for it were debts totalling $52,500. Well, Jakap was right about one thing, he did feel worse, much worse.

After what seemed like at least half an hour, but was probably only minutes, Jakap spoke again.

"OK, I would like you all to stand up, walk round the room and congratulate everyone else in the room."

At this point Dan spoke up:

"I don't wish to sound rude or disruptive at this stage, Jakap, but you have just highlighted the fact that I have earned over a million bucks during my working life and all I have to show for it is the possibility of some equity from my property. This, at some later date, may get me out of debt and leave me with a few dollars in my pocket if I get the timing of the property market right. That is nothing for people to congratulate me on."

Alex was beginning to really warm to Dan; he was not afraid to stand up and be counted, or to make the point that everyone else was thinking but were certainly too self-conscious to say out loud.

"I am so glad you said that, Dan, because I am sure that you are not the only person in the room who is thinking along those lines.

The reason that you should be congratulating each other is that you have all taken the first step to financial healing. By signing up for this course and actually turning up, you are doing something that we all must do if we want to make a change and that is to …"

With that, he walked over to his flip chart and wrote in large letters:

TAKE RESPONSIBILITY FOR YOUR ACTIONS

"Stephen Richards, author of *Think Your Way to Success: Let Your Dreams Run Free*, once said:

'The discontent and frustration that you feel is entirely your own creation.'

"This is the first real step to taking control of your finances. But be warned, the next few minutes contain some tough love.

"Firstly, you need to stop blaming other people and events for the financial situation in which you find yourself.

"I am guessing that up until this point, you have been saying things to yourself like 'things will get better when the next credit card is paid off' or 'I will start saving when I get my next pay rise.'

"Let me be blunt about this one – if you are thinking this, then you are just deluding yourself!

"How many of you have heard the phrase, 'If you keep on doing what you have always done, you will always get what you have always got'?

"Sometimes this pattern is easier to see in others close to you, rather than yourself. I am sure that you can think of someone who keeps repeating the same patterns in some element of their life, and expects different results."

Alex didn't need to think of anyone else.

Jakap continued, "It seems to me that there are three options: you can either do nothing about your situation and blame others or take responsibility for your actions.

"Complaining really is a waste of time. In general, we only actually complain about things that we can actually do something about.

"Remember when the world was supposed to end on 12 December 2012? People didn't complain; in fact it was a source of numerous jokes. My favourite being about the woman who asked everyone who thought the world was going to end if she could have all their Christmas presents as they wouldn't be needing them.

"When the world didn't end, it wasn't widely celebrated. Instead, people complained about the cost of Christmas as they spent far too much on presents that weren't needed, food that got thrown away, and parties where all that was left for blowing a week's salary was a hangover!

"Look, I don't want to come across all Scrooge-like over Christmas. It is just that Christmas is a prime example of the public being sucked in by the media and advertisers into buying this year's must-have present, completely over spending and having little or no control over our finances.

"Rant over!

"Taking responsibility for your actions can actually be very empowering. The day you decide that enough is enough, accept where you are, draw a line under it and decide to make that change is the day that you are no longer the victim! So let's celebrate that fact."

When Alex returned to his seat after congratulating every delegate, it was with a mixture of excitement and trepidation. Was he finally on his way to finding abundance, or was this yet another false dawn?

Jakap stood up.

"Well done for today. There was a lot of tough love and I promise that things will be a lot better from here. I just want to reassure you that I have been in the position where some, if not all, of you find yourselves now. I feel so blessed to be able to share with you the best bits of what I have learned after years of research, and a few dollars spent. Actually, make that many thousands of dollars spent!

"Tomorrow, I will share with you the one word that dictates why you don't have the abundance you want. Have a great evening everyone!"

Alex agreed to meet up with Dan and a few of the other delegates and then returned to his room. "I am going to have to write down the salient points from today whilst I can just about remember in which order they came," he thought.

Alex started typing:

Day 1 – Lessons Learned

- Although money is important, it is not the most important thing.
- Money alone will not buy me happiness.
- There are many people I know who have money but are not happy.
- I also know people with little or no money, but who are always smiling and seem contented.
- What money can provide is security. This will cause me far less stress in the workplace and in life in general.
- I have taken the first steps towards being abundant.
- I am taking responsibility for my actions and will no longer be making excuses.
- My current position is down to me, but this is where I draw the line, accept what is, and move forward.

Mark Bristow

4 LITTLE BY LITTLE

Jakap introduced Day Two. "Good morning and welcome back. It is great to see that everyone has returned today. Actually, I will let you into a little secret: everyone always comes back on Day Two."

Jakap was somewhat underplaying the enthusiasm in the room. Everyone was eagerly waiting to be financially "healed".

The main topic of conversation at dinner the previous evening had been Jakap himself: he seemed to be entirely confident that he could help everyone, without once appearing arrogant or ego driven. For many, this was indeed a pleasant change from the previous seminars they had attended, where it seemed to be more about the presenter and what he or she could sell you, rather than the actual content. Jakap was different, he certainly appeared to be someone whom you could trust and who really wanted to help. In short, he was someone you would want as a friend.

Jakap continued …

"Today, as promised, I am going to share with you the reason I believe you don't have the abundance you desire. Yesterday, we established your current financial position and for many of you, this made for uncomfortable reading. It is my guess that this may not be the first time you have addressed this issue. You have probably bought books, DVDs, CDs and have even attended other courses during which you have picked up a ton of useful techniques that you could use to bring you a life of abundance.

"So why don't you do it …?

"Before I answer that question, let's look at the last piece of pre-coursework I set you. This is where we look at where you are currently spending your money, and how one small change can make a huge difference.

"Who is prepared to share with the rest of the group how they spend their money?"

Alex raised his hand.

"OK Alex, thanks for volunteering. Now, I don't need to know everything you have written down, but just let me ask you this: do you buy yourself a coffee on the way to work each day?"

"Yes, I do."

"And do you have anything to eat with that?"

"Er, yes, usually a brownie."

"And, on average, how many dollars does that cost?"

"About five dollars."

"And do you go out and buy your lunch each day from a sandwich shop?"

"Yes, I do"

"And, again in dollars, how much does that cost?"

Alex started to smile, "Well, I usually go for a meal deal, so that is only six dollars."

"OK, so that is a total of eleven dollars for your coffee, brownie and lunch per day. So, if you waited until you got into work before having a coffee, passed on the brownie, and made your lunch at home, how much do you think that would cost you?"

"Probably no more than a dollar a day."

"So what we are saying here is that you could save yourself ten dollars a day, that is fifty dollars a week, $200 a month, assuming you work a five-day week."

"Yes, that seems correct."

"OK, bear with me a second."

Jakap then walked over to his computer and brought up a compound interest calculator, and proceeded to type in some figures.

"So, $200 a month, shall we see what the effect is over ten years, assuming, say, a seven per cent ongoing rate of increase?"

"Seems like a reasonable assumption," replied Alex.

"Right, over ten years, your savings would have grown to $34,818! OK, just for fun, give me a guess as to what the figure would be over twenty years."

"About $100,000?"

"Not bad, but of course you work in financial services. The actual figure is $104,793. If we were to increase the payments each year by say five per cent to take into account the increased cost of your coffee and lunch, the final figure would increase to ..."

"$154,955.47!!

"Let's break this down and explain step by step:

"Step1 – Alex spends ten minutes each day, making his own lunch rather than queuing in the coffee shop, saving himself $200 a month.

"Step 2 – Alex invests the money he saves into an investment that grows at seven per cent per year.

"Step 3 – Each year, Alex increases his regular payment by just five per cent to take into account the extra he would have had to pay in increased lunch and coffee cost.

"Step 4 – After twenty years, Alex would have accumulated $154,955.47.

"So that is over $150,000 for ten minutes work a day."

Stunned silence.

"So let's say that Alex didn't want to risk any of his savings at all. Instead, he puts the money in a safe in his house. It gets no growth or interest. Over the twenty years he would have accumulated over $79,000."

More stunned silence.

"By the way, doesn't that exercise also highlight the necessity to start doing something straight away rather than waiting a few years? Even if you don't increase the payments the bottom line is $104,793 over twenty years for a total investment of $48,000 against $34,818 over ten years, total invested $24,000.

"In other words, an additional $69,975 (104,793 – 34,818) for an additional outlay of only $24,000.

"OK, so that is an example of how a small change now can make a huge difference in the long term. Now, the harsh reality for most of you is that any money that you save by cutting down on your spending won't go into saving. Rather more, you should be using any additional funds to pay down any credit cards or loans.

"This is because the interest you will be paying on the outstanding balance is likely to be more than the seven per cent interest you would get from investing.

"So let's see how this small change will affect you."

Jakap opened another calculating tool on his computer entitled "The Loan Calculator".

"Let's suppose you owe $10,000 on a credit card and currently pay $200 a month towards paying down the debt. Assuming a realistic interest rate of fifteen per cent, it will take you seventy-nine months, which is over six and a half years, to pay off the total debt.

"And here is the real stinger …

"The total interest you will pay is $5,700!!

"Now it would be very glib of me to stand here and say 'don't build up credit card loans', but the reality is, and I have been in this position, is that for most of you in the room, a credit card balance of around $10,000 isn't out of the ordinary. So let's start to do something about it.

"Now if you are like Alex and can save an extra ten dollars a day by not buying lunch and coffee out, this is the effect it can have if you use the money saved each month to pay down the credit card. So, now, you are paying $400 a month instead of $200.

"The loan is repaid in thirty-one months, rather than seventy-nine and the interest payments total just over $2,000 instead of $5,700.

"So at the end of thirty-one months, you now have $400 to invest each month which consists of the original $200 you were using to pay down the credit card, together with the $200 per month you saved by making your own lunch and coffee.

"Let's say we invested that $400 for forty-eight months (to make it equate to the original period of seventy-nine months to pay off the credit card) at a growth rate of seven per cent each year, and you have accumulated savings of …

"$22,212!!"

Jakap turned the page over on his flip chart.

"I realise that I may have lost some of you there, so here is a brief summary:

Scenario 1

Credit card balance	$10,000
Interest rate	15%
Monthly payments	$200
Balance after 79 months	$0
Excess savings	$0

Scenario 2

Credit card balance	$10,000	
Interest rate	15%	
Savings interest rate	7%	
Monthly payments	$400	
Balance after 79 months	$0	(card paid off after 31 months)
Excess savings	$22,212	($400 invested for 48 months)

"So, small changes can make a big long-term difference. Now, who is going to start making their own lunch?" Jakap said with a smile.

"OK, so now I want you to look at your own expenditure lists and see where you can make your own small changes. Then, after lunch, I will share with you the one thing that stops you from having the abundance that you all want."

"Talk about leaving us wanting more," whispered Dan. "This is worse than the ending of an episode of *Homeland*. Forget lunch, just tell us what it is."

Alex chuckled, "I've waited long enough to hear this, I am guessing that another couple of hours won't make any difference."

That day, Alex went off to buy his lunch, wondering whether he would be making his own when he returned home. Although at this moment he really wanted to make the change, would he feel the same in a week's time when the euphoria of the course had died down and he was back in the "real" world?

Fortunately for Alex, he was not going to have to wait too long to find out.

For now, he was happy to live in the moment, full of expectation and excitement. In an attempt to capture how he was feeling, he noted in his phone the lessons learned from the morning session.

Lessons Learned:

- Little changes over a period can make a significant difference.
- Small regular savings over a long period can make a huge positive impact on your net worth.
- Make it a priority to pay off debts as soon as possible.
- This could be worth thousands in the long run.
- Do it now!
- Delaying costs money!

Mark Bristow

5 MONEY

Thank you for returning so promptly. I don't know why but everyone seems to get back on time for this session," said Jakap smiling.

"I am genuinely excited about what I am going to share with you this afternoon. Personally, when I 'got' this, my whole outlook on life shifted. Before I share with you what is the biggest barrier stopping you getting the abundance you desire, I just want to reassure some of you.

"What I am about to share is based upon the experience of running this course over 200 times. You are all at different stages in your own particular journey when you start this course and as a result will find that different elements will hold more relevance.

"For some, an exercise early on in the course may provide you with a 'light bulb' or 'aha' moment. Indeed, this may have already happened. For others, it may come much later, when you review your course notes or watch the DVD of the event.

"So, if your personal 'eureka' moment doesn't come straight away, be patient, it will come.

"OK, I think I have made you wait long enough for what is the one thing that dictates everything we do. This is a game changer.

"That one thing is ...

"BELIEF

"Henry Ford once said:

'Whether you believe you can or you can't, you are right.'

"OK, let's start at the very beginning.

"The dictionary describes belief as:
- an acceptance that something exists or is true, especially one without proof;
- something one accepts as true or real; a firmly held opinion;
- a religious conviction.

"I like to think of a belief as something that's engrained in you. It's a feeling of certainty that something is true. Successful people believe that they will be successful and will put in the hard work to make sure that their belief becomes a truth.

"Now I don't know much about soccer (or football, as our friends from the United Kingdom call it), but I do like to study successful people and so I was fascinated when David Beckham came to play in the USA.

"I discovered that he was never the most technically gifted player. However, he believed that by practising his techniques long after everyone else had left the training field, he could achieve his dream to play for England. Not only did he achieve that dream, he became one of the most well-known footballers on the planet.

"Probably the most famous basketball player of all time, Michael Jordan, once said 'I've always believed that if you put in the work, the results will come.'

"What many perceive to be a God-given talent is in fact a combination of talent, hard work and in-built belief that the hard work will lead to success. His list of achievements is a testimony to that.

"Beliefs strongly influence behaviour. If you truly believe something, you will take the action, like Michael Jordan and David Beckham, to make sure that belief becomes the truth.

"However, beliefs come with a downside, in that they can be negative as well as positive. In order to discover how beliefs are created, let's spend a little time looking at how your mind works.

"The mind has two levels, the conscious and the subconscious.

"The conscious mind is where we think logically based upon facts and is the mind of reason. If you are aware of what you are doing, you are likely to be doing it consciously.

"Your conscious mind is responsible for:
- Short-term memory
- Willpower
- Judgments and decisions
- Planning

"The second level, the subconscious, is far more powerful than your conscious mind. It is responsible for all your automatic body functions such as breathing, digestion and regulating your heart rate. If we didn't have a subconscious, we would have to learn how to walk again every day, for example.

"It is important to remember that the primary role of the subconscious is to protect you, and therefore beliefs are created with protection in mind.

"This is just the start of the process.

"I really recommend that if you haven't done so, you seek out the work of Bruce Lipton, who is a leader in the relatively new science of epigenetics. If ever you wanted to see someone who is passionate about his work and his beliefs, then look up him up on YouTube.

"In his excellent book, *The Biology of Belief*, he has calculated that at least ninety-five per cent of what we do, we do subconsciously. Therefore, if there is a conflict between the subconscious and the conscious mind, in the long term the subconscious will win.

"If you need an example to highlight this, think of diets. For most people, diets don't work in the long term because there is normally a negative belief running in the subconscious associated with always being overweight. Willpower is a conscious thinking process that for the most part will be superseded by a negative subconscious belief.

"For the successful dieters, there is always a belief change that comes with the weight loss. It isn't just about the weight loss, it is about what the successful weight loss proves.

"It is only when your subconscious beliefs change that long-term changes can be made.

"Your subconscious mind is responsible for:
- Automatic body functions
- Long-term memory
- Emotions
- Creativity
- Habits and patterns
- Protection

"If your mind were an army, the conscious would be the general, with the subconscious being the privates taking orders from the general, without being able to question those orders. If the wrong orders are sent to the army they still have to act on those orders.

"Like an army, the subconscious' primary role is that of protection, but if given incorrect orders, it will accept those orders as being true and will act accordingly.

"It is imperative, therefore, to ensure, that the orders that you give your subconscious are of a positive nature.

"So how are beliefs created?

"When we were born, we knew how to express ourselves whenever and wherever we wanted. Our mind was like a brand new computer without any programs loaded. As time progresses, we take on the beliefs and realities of others around us and, in effect, our 'computer' starts to load other people's programs.

"The reason for this is that up to the age of six, we have no conscious mind to speak of, which means that there is no filter system in place deciding whether the beliefs that we take on from others are actually applicable to us.

"Having no apparent conscious mind often means that we look at events in an illogical way. When I was four years old, my parents took me on my first trip to New York. Whilst we were in Bloomingdales one day, I got lost. Now although I was probably only lost for a matter of minutes, it was enough for me to create a belief that I was alone and unloved by my parents.

"This belief was created because my parents, instead of giving me a hug when they found me, told me off for running away.

"Now looking back on that event on a conscious level, the thought of my parents not loving me couldn't be further from the truth. I had the best upbringing I could have wished. My parents were always supportive and I never wanted for anything, yet this one incident was enough to create a negative belief that hindered me for a good part of my life.

"Once a belief is created, we look for evidence to support this belief. Those of you who have read *The Secret* or similar books will be aware of the Law of Attraction."

Dan interrupted, "Yeah, this Law of Attraction stuff. Well I have read *The Secret* and it basically says 'decide what you want, tell the universe what you want, and the universe will give it back to you'. Well I have tried this hundreds of times and it has only worked about twice, and I am putting those down to luck."

"Dan, thank you for making that particular point, I am sure that you have just said what a lot of people may be thinking. My take on it is this:

"I think that the Law of Attraction does work but only if your beliefs are congruent with what you are trying to attract. For example, if you are trying to manifest your dream house by using the Law of Attraction, but you have a subconscious belief that you don't deserve to have abundance, there is a lack of congruence and the negative belief will always be the winner. I also believe that you have to put some work in to ensure that your visions become reality.

"There is further bad news in that the Law of Attraction also works in a negative way, looking to support the initial negative beliefs that you created. If a compass on a ship is set just a couple of degrees incorrectly and continues on that path, it can end up miles away from its chosen destination. Similarly, if you start with a slightly incorrect belief, it can lead to you being a long way from where you want to be in life.

"Our beliefs will totally affect how we look at things, whether the glass is half empty or half full. They affect our behaviour and how we view life. They create our own map of the world.

"A gargantuan insight I was given early in my own journey was that everyone has their own map of the world and the map is not the territory.

"The map is not the territory," he repeated.

"When I was told, I must admit that it took a little while to comprehend, but 'WOW' when I did, what a difference it made in my life. I had always been told that everyone is different, but this took it to a much deeper level: a profound statement, yet so simple.

"Our behaviour is based upon our own experiences and the lessons that those experiences have told us, in other words: our beliefs dictate our behaviour.

"This is absolutely huge. In order to understand other people properly, we need to look at their map of the world, to look at life through their eyes.

"When I was ten years old, I was at a small-town school. In tests, I always came second or third in class. There was one boy, Stefan Lawson, who always came first. He also happened to be good on the sports field and a nice guy, so I couldn't even dislike him, although I was jealous of him.

"In the end of year exam, however, I came top; I had finally beaten Stefan. After spending years in his shadow, when it really mattered, I had beaten him.

"So how did I celebrate? Well, the sad answer is that I didn't, despite my parents showering me with praise. I just thought I must have been extremely lucky and maybe Stefan had had a bad day.

"So why did I react in this way? The simple answer is that I was running a belief that I wasn't good enough. The belief I created when I got lost in Bloomingdales six years earlier.

"So, what can we conclude about this? (Other than don't take a four-year-old shopping in Bloomingdales.) Well, if you are running negative beliefs about money, those beliefs probably started at a very early age and could have originated from a number of sources, such as:

- Parents
- Grandparents
- Brothers and sisters
- Teachers
- Friends
- TV
- Movies
- Newspapers
- Songs

"Whilst your initial beliefs may have been passed down from parents, grandparents, brothers, sisters and teachers, further evidence to support your beliefs may have come from TV, films, newspapers, songs etc.

"Do any of you remember your parents or grandparents making statements such as 'Money doesn't grow on trees' or 'I am not made of money'?

"How often have you watched a movie or a TV programme where the bad guys are rich and use their financial position to manipulate and use others?

"Looking around the room, I am guessing that a few of you were around in the eighties, although of course you were very, very young," he laughed. "Well one of the programmes with the highest ratings in that decade was *Dallas*. For those of you who watched the show, can you remember how it portrayed rich people?"

"They are ruthless and power mad with no feelings for others," said a well-dressed lady called Katy who had described herself as a "well-paid but penniless attorney".

"And don't even get me started on how most of the women in that programme were portrayed."

"In that case we won't," smiled Jakap, "but can you see how the programme would certainly help to reinforce any negative beliefs you may have about wealth and rich people? If the initial belief is present, there is always a lot of evidence around to support it.

"Now is a good time to introduce you to Anita. I met Anita a couple of years ago and now she helps me with these courses, as well as working and dealing with clients on a one-to-one basis. Anita, would you like to share your story?"

Anita stood up, she was a bubbly person with the broadest smile that Alex had ever seen and looked to the outside world like she never had a problem in her life.

"Hi everyone, well my story today is quite short really. When I was growing up, I was always told to be wary of my uncle Elmo. He was ruthless and not a very nice man at all. He certainly wasn't to be trusted.

"He also happened to be very wealthy. Only recently, I realised that I based myself upon Uncle Elmo; I had created the belief that in order to be wealthy, you had to be ruthless and were not to be trusted. Therefore I tried to keep my distance from anyone who had money. Despite this, I seemed to make friends with people who had money. And guess what? The friends with money were the least trustworthy. It got to the stage where the more money they had the less I could trust them.

"Now that I have realised this link, I have now broken my ties with those I can't trust and my life is a whole lot better for having done so.

"My previous beliefs around wealth have meant that every time I made money I haven't kept it for very long because this little voice inside of me would be saying that I was about to turn into a horrible person, and I didn't want that.

"Crazy when you think about it. But I lived like that for over thirty years, before my own 'light bulb' moment."

"Thank you for sharing, Anita. I now want to concentrate on the screen where we should see another friend of mine, Angela. We met on an external course and I know that she won't mind me reminding her that she was the shrinking violet in the corner, looking extremely troubled and certainly not the vibrant person you see up on the screen before you today. What I didn't know was that she was suffering financial difficulties which made her feel that she was carrying the weight of the world on her shoulders."

Jakap turned to the screen.

"Angela, thank you for connecting with us today and sharing your story, how did your bad relationship with money begin?"

"Thank you for that introduction, Jakap.

"Well, my story starts as a young girl. I always used to save part of my pocket money and put it in a little pile on a table next to my bed. The problem was that my mother used to take money from the pile to pay for groceries. Consequently, I formed the belief that I would never hold on to money and I have struggled to do so ever since. Any time I had money, I was literally giving it away. This thread carried on throughout my life, even to the extreme of marrying someone who took me to bankruptcy."

"My mother also told me that 'money was for others and not for the likes of us' and just further enhanced my negative beliefs around money.

"Finally, Mother always told me that you had to 'work hard for the money'. This is currently something that still holds me back to an extent. You see what I really want to do is help as many people as I can but be paid for it. This is where my passion lies and I believe it is my true vocation.

"When I do this type of work, I find it difficult to charge a realistic fee because it doesn't feel like hard work at all. I still have my mother in my head saying 'you have to work hard for the money'. Invariably, I have found employment where I have had to work hard for little or no enjoyment.

"It is only now that I realise that you can do what you love for a living and get paid for doing it. It definitely isn't hard work; it is the thing that makes me feel the most alive."

"Thank you Angela, for your honesty and sharing. You are an inspiration to us all. Now, it is time to give a big cheer for Lena who is going to share her story."

Lena, a slim lady who dressed in bright colours and had the personality to match, stepped forward. The energy in the room increased dramatically as she started to speak.

"Well, I want to begin by saying how spookily close my story is to that of Angela's. My grandparents came to America from Jamaica and my grandfather always said that money was always hard to come by and that it 'wasn't for the likes of us, it was for them'. It was quite a while before I found out who 'them' were. Because my mother was brought up in the environment of scarcity, she never had any money and would often take money from my little pile of savings.

"This created a belief that money wouldn't stay with me for long. I would always spend money as soon as I received it, and I would spend it all, because if I didn't, my mother would take it.

"Even as recently as six months ago, as soon as I got money, I would spend it, and mainly on things that I already had and certainly didn't need. I mean, I have twenty mugs, when will I ever need twenty mugs? I can't even get twenty people in my house at one time, I only have four chairs!

"I am also slightly ashamed to say that if my partner ever leaves any loose change around the house, I take it and have it for myself!

"All this behaviour is mainly because I adopted the beliefs of my grandparents and my mother. Now I have realised this, I am working hard to change those beliefs.

"Thank you for listening to my little story."

"No, thank you Lena and, of course, Anita and Angela, I think you will agree that the stories we have heard today are prime examples that small experiences as a child can have big consequences, and I am guessing that these stories resonate with some of you.

"We are learning a lot today so let's summarise. I am hoping that from the stories you have heard today you understand why we need to spend some time on beliefs.

"Your beliefs form you and will run your life.

"So if you believe that you are going to be successful …

"Then you will do what is necessary to ensure that it happens.

"If you believe you're not going to be successful you will sub-consciously find evidence to support that belief.

"OK, so with this in mind, let's find out your beliefs towards money and wealth. We are going to do this as an exercise in pairs. I want you to pair up with someone who you haven't worked with before."

Jakap walked over to the flipchart.

"Here are the questions I want you to ask each other.

"Which sayings about wealth, money or being rich do you remember from your childhood? To assist you, here is the list of potential sources:

- Parents
- Grandparents
- Brothers and sisters
- Teachers
- Friends
- TV
- Movies
- Newspapers
- Songs

"Once you have answered that question, consider these:

"What is your current attitude towards wealth or money?

"What do you think is required in order to get rich?

"What do you think about rich people?"

Alex chose to work with a quiet man named Martin, an IT consultant based in Boston. Back in the eighties, he had earned a lot of money when the demand for computer expertise was at a premium. Like many of his ilk, he would quite happily describe himself as 'a bit of a geek', which he carried over to an obsession with music and Apple products.

"To be honest, I don't remember any discussions about money when I was growing up, which kind of makes me stuck on the first question."

"Hang on, didn't you say you were heavily into music? Perhaps there are some songs that you remember that were about money?"

"Well most of my teenage years were spent listening to *Dark Side of the Moon* by Pink Floyd on a daily basis. Probably the most famous track is 'Money'. I guess the line that really stands out is the one that says: 'but if you ask for a rise it's no surprise that they're giving none away', although I am thinking that is hardly likely to generate any positive beliefs about finances."

"No, I think you may have a point there," replied Alex. "The songs that I remember were 'money, money, money, must be funny, in a rich man's world.' Then there was Simply Red stating that 'money's too tight to mention.' For some reason, they have stuck in my mind."

Martin thought for a few seconds. "Yes, I do remember them vaguely, although you would have to be a bit of a geek like me because most people this side of the pond wouldn't. I wonder if there was ever a song that was really positive about money. Even if there are any, they are sure outnumbered by the negative ones. I bet there isn't a blues song that starts with 'Woke up this morning, I had won the lottery!'

"The same could be said of newspapers," he continued. "They seem to take great delight in highlighting the wrongdoings of the rich and famous, rather than the great charitable donations by the likes of

Richard Branson, J. K. Rowling and many more. I guess bad news sells."

Martin continued by saying that money was not that important to him, which took Alex aback slightly. So he asked Martin, in the nicest possible way, "Why are you on the course if you feel that way?"

"Well I am very organised and I have control over everything I do, except money. I have wasted so much money on having the most up-to-date gadgets available and I don't really understand why. Most of them, I haven't used more than two or three times.

"In the eighties, when I was earning big bucks, it wasn't important as I had money to burn, but times have changed. So, although money isn't important, not wasting money is!

"I have wondered a million times why I keep buying all these gadgets, and it is really getting to me. I haven't got the answer; I don't have control over the situation, so it is time to seek help."

Martin moved onto the remaining questions. In order to get rich, he suggested that you needed to be ruthless, single minded and willing to walk over others. Having discussed his answers with Alex, he conceded that this was hardly the right mind-set to have if he ever wanted a positive bank balance.

It was now Alex's turn. His only memory from his childhood was his dad saying once that "money doesn't grow on trees". However, growing up, he never wanted for anything; the family had great holidays and he always got what he wanted at Christmas and for his birthday.

His current attitude towards money was a bit "easy come, easy go". Whenever he was in financial difficulty, his parents had always bailed him out and even since his father died, his attitude had not changed. This left him feeling totally uneasy, to the extent that he thought he was going to be physically sick. After all, he spent his working day telling people the importance of planning (he remembered seeing a business card that read "No one plans to fail, they just fail to plan"), of regular saving and of making this a priority.

"Cobbler's shoes," he thought to himself.

Alex looked at the remaining questions. "I have a bit of a dilemma when it comes to describing rich people because of the J. K. Rowling factor."

"What do you mean by that?" enquired Martin.

"I think that you need to be focused and determined and not to care what other people think about you. But then there is J. K. Rowling. Whilst she is obviously focused and determined, she certainly cares about people. It is estimated that she has given away $160 million of her fortune and that is the main reason she fell out of the Forbes rich list. She isn't the only one, there are others, like Richard Branson and George Lucas, who have done great work for charity.

"Now, I am really confused. The only conclusion I can arrive at is that the 'money doesn't grow on trees' comment from Dad just overrides everything, which just seems incredibly frustrating."

Alex didn't have time to ponder the situation further, because at that moment Jakap stood up and began to summarise.

"OK guys, if this exercise uncovered a number of negative beliefs around money and wealth for you, then congratulate yourself. You have taken some important steps on the path towards having control of your finances. And if you haven't uncovered any negative beliefs around money, congratulate yourself, as you are also one step closer towards being in control of your finances.

"Hold on there, big fella," Dan quipped. "That just doesn't make sense. If we haven't uncovered anything, how can that be one step closer?"

"Can I remind you of a quote attributed to Thomas Edison?

"'I have not failed. I've just found 10,000 ways that won't work.' If you haven't found any negative beliefs around money, you are one step closer to finding out what it is that you have negative beliefs around.

"And that, my friends, is where we end for the day."

Alex returned to his room and wrote down the main points from the afternoon session.

Summary of the Afternoon Session

- There is a direct correlation between your beliefs about money and wealth, and your current financial position.
- My beliefs were created when I was young and are based on my surroundings and environment.
- Beliefs are held in the subconscious, which acts to protect. However, these beliefs may no longer be relevant.

6 I STILL HAVEN'T FOUND WHAT I'M LOOKING FOR

W ell I hope you found yesterday's session useful," commenced Jakap at the start of the morning session, "even if it may have been a little frustrating for some!

"This morning I want to introduce you to the work of my favourite inspirational author, Dr Wayne Dyer, and in particular his excellent book entitled *Excuses Be Gone*. If you live in the UK, the book is entitled *No More Excuses*.

"This book asks you to question your beliefs head-on and question the viability of those beliefs.

"So yesterday, you may have written something like ...'I am no good with money'. But is that actually true? Can any of you think of occasions when you have been good with money? Any volunteers to answer that one?"

"Well, I saved enough money to put down a deposit for the house I purchased," offered a middle-aged lady named Nadia.

"And have you saved for anything else?"

"Well I always save up for my holidays and my children's college funds and presents for them, I always saved for them."

"So straightaway you have come up with three examples of why your belief around money is wide of the mark," Jakap interjected. "Could it be that this belief is, in fact, just an excuse and that there is little evidence to support this?

"So what if we spin this on its head and write the opposite to what you have previously written. Let's write 'I am good with money'.

"In fact, write it out three times and say it aloud, or to yourself a hundred times and see how that feels."

At this point, Alex's heart sank a little. The idea that his beliefs about money and abundance may have little actual evidence to support them – this was something he was quite happy to explore. But to list the opposite and then say it out loud a hundred times seemed to be just an extension of the "think positive and everything will be brilliant" philosophy that he had read a thousand times.

"Now I know some of you will be thinking 'I have done something like this a thousand times'," Jakap continued, "but just try it, please just try it. What have you got to lose?"

"What indeed?" laughed Alex as he momentarily contemplated whether Jakap was a mind-reader and that Richard had been right about Harry all along.

So he tried it …

And after he tried it, he was left feeling slightly intrigued. It certainly hadn't changed his life in the way he had hoped. In his dreams, there would be a sudden shaft of light shining on him from on high, like in the church scene from *The Blues Brothers* when Jake has his "enlightenment moment" and realises that he needs to get the band back together.

No, there was no divine intervention, but he did feel slightly better, something that hadn't happened when he had previously tried positive thinking.

"Now imagine if you did that three times a day, every day, for at least twenty-one days, do you think that will change things?"

Even though there appeared to be general agreement around the room, Dan stepped up and asked the question on everyone's lips.

"So, Jakap, are you saying that is all we need to do? Just keep repeating the same thing until it is embedded in our brain – that is all we need to do? For years I have been looking for an answer, and it is just … that?"

"No, Dan, if only it were that easy for all of us, but for some of you it just may be.

"So for now, I want you to go back to your list of beliefs and write the opposite. Then look for the evidence to support this opposite belief and then say it either out loud or to yourself one hundred times."

Alex looked at his list, the first belief read: "I am not made of money."

The opposite did not seem to make sense, so he decided to tweak it slightly to read, "I can make money easily". Then he asked himself whether that statement was true. Well, yes, it was. Everywhere he had worked, he had made money easily. Basically, all he had to do was turn up, do the work and he got paid.

The trouble was that he spent everything he earned, and then some!

Alex continued through the rest of his list and rewrote his beliefs. As he looked at his rewrites, he came to the overriding conclusion that making money was not the problem: keeping it was.

This was a mini-breakthrough for Alex. In his role as an advisor, he had always been coached to ask plenty of questions of his clients in order to get to the core of their problem so that he could come up with the most appropriate solution.

By "drilling down" he had realised that the big problem wasn't necessarily that he didn't make enough money; it was that he couldn't hang on to it. Instead of saving on a regular basis, he was always looking for the quick fix, the dream investment that was going to make him a million overnight.

He had come so far but still had not reached the breakthrough that he was looking for. He was in a pensive mood when the session broke for lunch.

There were just one and a half days left of the workshop. "Would there be enough time to reach the end of the path?" he asked himself. As he sat down to write his notes from the session, just one sentence seemed to cover it all.

Morning Session Notes

- The problem is not how to make money; it is how to keep it!

7 MAN IN THE MIRROR

W elcome back to the afternoon session," Jakap said. "We have started our diagnosis, but there is a lot more work to be done.

"It may feel like someone has given you a headache pill to try to cure your migraine. The pill may have eased the pain a little, but the migraine is still there.

"So far, we have looked at your negative beliefs around money and abundance. So would now be a good time to reveal what most books, courses etc fail to tell you?"

"Indeed it would," thought Alex.

"OK, here it is …

"It is not just your beliefs about money that stop you from having what you want financially …

"It is the beliefs you hold about yourself!

"Remember the story I told earlier about being lost in Bloomingdales. The negative belief created that day wasn't around money. However, for a long time, I held a belief that I wasn't good enough and didn't deserve abundance. This was reflected in my financial situation despite the fact that I held down well-paid jobs showing clients how to invest their money to make even more money!

"In other words, my financial situation was a direct reflection of the beliefs I held about myself. And it wasn't just my financial situation that was affected. If you are running subconscious beliefs that you are not good enough, this will be reflected in various areas of your life, for example, your relationship, your weight, your job as well as your finances.

"I managed to sabotage a number of potentially fantastic long-term relationships and was always carrying a few extra pounds and spending my working days in a job that wasn't my true vocation.

"My mission as Financial Healer is to help you change your self-worth in order to increase your net worth and to find your authentic self along the way. You have all the answers within; I just lend a helping hand.

"To emphasise the point that I have just made, I would now like to introduce you to Ally who is going to share her story."

Ally was a tall blond lady who stood very upright, but it hadn't always been that way. She recounted her story of how, as a result of an incident when she was three years old, she had created a belief that her parents didn't think she was good enough.

She had carried this belief into her adult life and married an alcoholic who continually told her that she was not worth anything. This was despite the fact that she had taken on his three children and brought them up as her own, as well as the two children they had had together. At the same time, she had her own café business. This involved running the café during the day, balancing the books at night and cooking the food for the next day. The business failed because her husband regularly stole the takings and spent them in the local bar.

Ally's negative beliefs were not around money as such; they

weren't the reason the business had failed – it was her overall belief about herself. She felt that she did not deserve money so every time money came into her life, it soon disappeared.

Ultimately, the stress of her lifestyle led her to suffering from chronic fatigue and fibromyalgia and she could barely stand at all.

Her negative belief ensured that all areas of her life were affected. Once she had identified the trigger, she took control of her life and made the necessary changes.

Jakap thanked Ally for sharing her story and congratulated her on her recovery.

"These negative beliefs become more powerful as the universe provides further evidence to support the initial belief.

"My point is that we need to dig deeper, to peel back more layers of the onion in order to uncover those negative beliefs that are holding you back. This next exercise requires you to be totally honest about yourself if you really want to make that change.

"I want you to take some paper, or your journal, and write the heading 'Negative Beliefs about Myself' and then list those beliefs.

"To help you pinpoint those negative beliefs, I am going to borrow an exercise from Greg Braden. This particular exercise I have taken from his contribution to the book and film *Choice Point*.

"Please write down the following questions:

"What negative behaviours do you see in your family, or in your workplace?

"What negative behaviours do you see in the world as a whole?

"Now before you say 'well what has this got to do with my negative beliefs, surely this is about other people?' I am going to quote Greg directly. This is what Greg has to say:

'If we see conflict around us — in our personal world of family, social, and work environments — or if conflict in the world occupies our attention, it might be mirroring a conflict in how we are living our lives compared to how we want to live our lives.'

"So, for example, if you have written down being angry or judgmental as being negative traits in other people, are they mirroring your anger and your judgment? Sometimes they might be. However, if the answer is no, then it is very possible they mirror what we actually judge in ourselves, i.e. we are angry and judgmental about ourselves.

"So to summarise Greg, what we see as being negative in others could be one of two things: a mirror of our own negative traits or a reflection of our negative internal dialogue.

"OK guys, enough talking from me, time for action."

As Alex wrote his list of negatives, he recognised a change. If someone had suggested he write this list only a week beforehand, he would have felt very uncomfortable indeed. Now it seemed an enlightening experience and he was actually looking forward to sharing his issues with like-minded people within an honest environment.

"Just write what immediately comes into your consciousness," Jakap had said. "There will be plenty of time to filter your answers later."

Once he had started writing, the negatives started to flow:

Negative Beliefs About Myself

- I will never be as good as Dad.
- I will never be as good as my work colleagues.
- I will never be in a long-term relationship and feel totally comfortable.
- I never do things on time.
- I never do things that show off my ability.

- I spend too much time on non-productive work.
- I spend too much time on the people that don't matter to the detriment of those that do.
- Although I am perceived as the guy who helps others, I am actually quite selfish.
- I have tunnel vision and I don't listen enough to others.
- I don't stand up for myself and am easily bullied.
- I am afraid to move out of my comfort zone.

As Alex looked down at his list, he realised he was not the only one; Dan was looking over his shoulder.

"Hell, you really are down on yourself, aren't you?"

"I guess I am," reflected Alex. "But you know what? Now I have written all this down, the line has been drawn. I know now where I am, what I need to work on, and what needs to change."

Dan interjected, "If a friend of yours was as hard on you, as you as are on yourself, then they probably wouldn't be your friend for much longer!"

Alex laughed, "Yes, Dan, you are probably right, although as I am, I would still speak to them because I wouldn't want to offend! How stupid is that?"

"About as stupid as it gets. Alex, despite what you have written, you are one of the good guys and deserve more respect. So I will ask again, you would never be this hard on anyone else so why be this hard on yourself?"

"Because, deep down, this is what I believe. This is my reality."

"So how do we go about changing your beliefs if they are that deeply embedded?"

"That is the $64,000 question."

Right on cue, Jakap brought the group back together.

"Tomorrow, we will look even deeper into your beliefs, add the final pieces of the jigsaw that will show you once and for all why you are the way you are, why it has been so difficult to change, and how you can now change, forever!

"Have a great evening, and be ready for some life-changing tomorrow!"

Alex did not go to the restaurant that evening; instead, he just grabbed a sandwich and returned to his room. The day had been full of harsh realities and his brain felt scrambled. He needed to be alone to collect his thoughts. He took out his journal.

Day 3 - Lessons Learned:

- Are my beliefs just excuses?
- Could the opposite belief be true?
- The beliefs about myself affect my financial position.
- Change your self-worth to improve your net worth.

8 YOU'RE MY BEST FRIEND

Alex woke early the next morning. The previous day had left him mentally exhausted and he had fallen to sleep around 8pm. Now, he felt the type of excitement that reminded him of when he was a six-year-old at Christmas, eagerly awaiting his first football kit. Was today going to be the day when he would finally blast through his money blocks and truly be on the path to abundance and happiness? He couldn't wait to start.

When he arrived at the workshop room it was empty and the flipchart had one word written on it. The word was:

SUBCONSCIOUS

As the remaining delegates entered, there was a noticeable buzz of anticipation which Alex likened to the build up at a concert waiting for the major act to appear. Finally, Jakap arrived.

"So we are getting towards the end of this workshop, time for some reflection. My aim today is to ensure that you are on the right path to what you ultimately want from life.

"Some words of warning. This path will have roadblocks along the way but there will be people in your life who will help remove those roadblocks.

"There will be days when you will question whether everything is worth all the hard work. On those days, look back down your path and reflect on just how far you have come. So many people go a long way down the right path only to turn back because it becomes a little difficult. Ultimately, they die with their song still in them. Isn't that sad?

"Bob Proctor once said:

'Your subconscious mind is giving you the direction to your goal. Many of the actions will require you to do things you are not in the habit of doing and old habits die hard. The old habits will fight back. You will be tested many times every day.'

"Let's make sure we reach our own destinations and have fun on the journey.

"We have established that it is our beliefs that create our relationship with money as well as in other areas of our life.

"We questioned our money beliefs on a conscious level, and for some, that may have already created a shift. I hope that when you return home, you will do the same exercise in respect of your other negative beliefs. For those of you who still hold negative beliefs around money, let's look closer at the subconscious.

"The Subconscious ...

"I like to think of the subconscious as a computer containing files of programmed beliefs that have been acquired from early childhood. Some programs continue to work well if updated from time to time but others attract viruses and need to be removed and replaced by updated programs.

"These programs were initially installed to offer protection. Unlike a computer, however, you are not normally offered automatic updates. Therefore, these old programs are still running even though they are not relevant to your current circumstances and will hinder overall performance.

"Earlier on, I mentioned that the subconscious mind runs most of your life. There is scientific proof that backs this up. From experiments conducted using MRI scanning, neuroscientists have calculated that the conscious mind can process information at forty bits per second whereas the unconscious can operate at forty million bits per second.

"Therefore, most of our decisions, actions, emotions and behaviour depend on the brain activity that is beyond our conscious awareness.

"Can you remember what it was like when you were first learning how to drive? You had to think of everything at a conscious level, such as checking the mirror, signalling, letting off the brake and then turning the wheel etc. Nowadays, you do all that without thinking about it consciously. Indeed, we talk to other passengers, listen to music and even have a hands-free telephone conversation.

"Your subconscious is there to protect you. It does this by storing information passed on from your conscious mind to be used in times of danger. For example, you wouldn't put your hand into an open fire because your subconscious has already decided that this would not be a good idea.

"But is the subconscious always helpful?

"As I have mentioned numerous times, your subconscious forms beliefs at a very early age. It then searches for evidence to support this belief. Our logical mind doesn't start developing until about the age of six and until that time, we are reliant upon those around us to provide us with the information we need.

"So if your parents have negative beliefs about money, it is fairly likely that these beliefs will be installed in you.

"But, before you go off to call your parents to blame them for your lack of wealth, I would like to share with you one of the fundamental teachings that I learned when studying Neuro Linguistic Programming (NLP) and that has stayed with me ever since.

"And that is ...

"People do whatever they do with a positive intention. It is possible for someone to have a positive intention whilst acting in a negative fashion. For example, you and I will have encountered people who make negative comments about others. Their positive intention is to make themselves look better by making others look less good.

"So looking at the negative beliefs that your parents had about money, what would be their positive intentions? In my experience, this falls into two categories:

"The first category concerns the beliefs that are passed down to our parents from their own parents. Often, these beliefs have never been questioned.

"Category two is that of protection. For many parents, security is deemed to be of paramount importance. The concept of security works on a number of levels but, often, creating abundance involves taking risks which the security conscious are unwilling to take.

"And of course, this stretches across all our beliefs, not just those around money. So what is it all really about? I believe that it all comes down to fear and love.

"In my one-to-one work, I have encountered clients with what appears to be many different issues. However, I believe when you peel back the layers of the onion, there are two main core beliefs: 'the world is a dangerous place' and 'I am not loved enough'.

"There are a number of variations on this which can essentially be condensed to:

- The world is a dangerous place
- Fear of failure
- Fear of success

"Consciously, fear of success seems illogical. After all, why would anyone not want to succeed? In reality though, there may be a whole number of reasons why success is to be feared.

"I am not loved or not deserving.

"We have heard plenty of examples of this over the last few days. How many stories are there of lottery winners who have won millions, only to have lost it all within a relatively short period of time?

"Those people were subconsciously running a program that says 'we are not deserving'.

"You may require some help with this, so let's bring in your best friend. You do know who your best friend is, don't you? It is your subconscious!"

"What? This same subconscious that keeps running these programs that stop me from getting rich? Some friend!" quipped Dan.

"Yes, the very same. But like all best friends, you have to tell him or her when they aren't making you happy. Also, like all best friends, your subconscious needs some TLC sometimes.

"So now I am going to share with you a neat little technique to create dialogue between your conscious and subconscious minds. This may seem a little crazy at first, but when you establish a good working relationship between your two minds, huge shifts can be made in a relatively short space of time.

"Let's start by talking to your subconscious, don't worry, you don't have to do this out loud, do it as if you were talking to another person. So here goes.

"First of all, thank your subconscious for all the help it has given you in the past and maybe apologise for neglecting it over the years.
"You might want to say something like 'thank you for everything

that you have done for me. I am sorry to have neglected you over the years but was wondering whether you would be willing to help me.'

"Now, we have to wait for our subconscious to acknowledge us. Acknowledgement can come in many different forms. When my subconscious acknowledges me, I get Rapid Eye Movement (REM) and for a while become a shiny happy person, bad joke for all you music fans, I know. Others have noted slight pressure in their solar plexus or a twitching in the fingers. It could be anything but you will know when it happens.

"This acknowledgement means that the subconscious is willing to help."

"Once you get the acknowledgement ...

"Ask for help. To test this out, work with something simple. When I first tried this technique, I had mislaid a set of keys. This was a real irritant as I felt that I had looked in every conceivable place they might be. So, although I thought this was stretching the boundaries somewhat of what I thought could be achieved (yes, I had those same doubts that you are probably having right now), I decided to try it out. After all, there was nothing to lose. So, what I did was to shut my eyes and say:

"'I have forgotten where I have left my keys, can you help me with this?'

"I got the rapid-eye-movement response and, over the next few days, I started getting the feeling that I should be looking in a specific wardrobe. I eventually found the keys in a jacket hanging in that wardrobe.

"The lesson I learned that day is not necessarily to expect a direct answer straightway, but to trust my subconscious to guide me to the right place.

"There is no hard and fast rule as to how co-operative your subconscious will be. Many of my clients run all major decisions past their subconscious and find that it is incredibly helpful.

"The subconscious is always trying to help, whether we listen or not. How many times have you said 'I wish I had trusted my gut feeling on this one'? That gut feeling was your subconscious at work.

"The subconscious for belief changing ...

"Once you have re-established a relationship with the subconscious, you can then start to work on belief changing. This is how it works:

1. Thank your subconscious for holding on to the beliefs that you want to change, and for the protection the beliefs have provided in the past.
2. State that the belief is no longer relevant and that a new, positive belief is needed to replace it.
3. Confirm with your subconscious that it is prepared to help.
4. Outline the new belief, and repeat the belief ten times.
5. On a regular basis, at least three times a day, repeat the belief to your subconscious.

"If you repeat steps 4 and 5 every day for twenty-one days, this should be sufficient to create your new belief. To further imprint your new belief, write it down and post it around your home to act as constant reminders.

"You may also want to record your new beliefs and then play these back to yourself first thing in the morning and last thing at night as you drift off to sleep.

"Try it on everything, you have nothing to lose.

"Having regular contact with your subconscious can help you in many ways. In particular, I find that I don't need to think through problems endlessly on a conscious level. Now, I pass the problem over to my subconscious and wait for it to come up with a solution.

"So let's practise talking to your subconscious and I will see you after lunch. Remember to bring your best friend with you!"

Alex returned to his journal:

Lunchtime Note

- Your subconscious is your best friend, use it.

9 ACTION THIS DAY

Welcome to the last afternoon of the workshop," Jakap began, "I hope that you are all wide awake because I have a great deal more I wish to share with you. We have spent a great deal of time concentrating on your subconscious, and rightly so. This afternoon, I want to share with you ideas you can work on with your subconscious to help you on your way to leading the life you want to lead. These ideas are based upon over twenty years of my own self-development and over $50,000 spent on courses, books, seminars workshops, DVDs and CDs. Does that sound good? Excellent! Let's do it.

"The first tip is to take responsibility for your actions. Your self-worth and net worth will only increase if you make that decision to make that change. You may have a hundred reasons or a hundred people to blame for why you are in your current financial situation. Whatever they are, from now on, it is down to you. No one else is going to give the energy you can give to this particular project, they are too busy dealing with their own stuff. When you leave this workshop, promise yourself that you will make that change.

"Tip number two is to stop being a people-pleaser! I am reminded of this quote from Pierce Brosnan:

'You can get totally messed up trying to please everyone with what you do, but ultimately, you have to please yourself.'

"There is a sure fire way to determine whether you value yourself highly enough. Just ask yourself the following question:

"'Am I a people-pleaser?'

"If the answer is yes ...

"Then you do not feel loved, or deserving enough.

"Now, before Dan takes me to task on this one," Jakap continued with a smile, "I am not advocating that you shouldn't help others, far from it. Some of the greatest people who have ever lived on this planet spent their lives helping others. My definition of 'people-pleasers', are those who always put others first, usually to their own detriment and to the detriment of those closest to them.

"A huge part of this journey is learning to love ourselves. The first step in this is to forgive yourself for anything that you may have done in your past. We have all made mistakes in the past. You can't change that. It is time to draw a line and to move on. Maria Robinson once said:

'Nobody can go back and start a new beginning, but anyone can start today and make a new ending.'

"I want to talk about Katie. Although only nineteen, she had spent most of her life trying to please her father. The only time she appeared to get his recognition was when she was running. Obviously, as we all know, in order to be good at running it certainly helps if you are not carrying excess weight. When a friend made a throw-away comment to the effect that if she didn't exercise, she would become fat, Katie took her keeping-slim regime to a dangerous level. She exercised so much and ate so little that her weight dropped to seventy-three pounds, and in her own words she was 'one week away from death'.

"During our sessions, Katie realised that Dad wasn't able to provide emotional support but could provide practical help. She stopped trying to please him and accepted that he would be around for the practical things in life.

"She also realised that she had all the emotional support she needed from her mother who provided it in abundance.

"From that moment of realisation, Katie began to love herself for who she was.

"Katie's dad wasn't a bad person. He just had his own stuff going on that prevented him from providing the emotional support that she craved. When she started to love herself, she realised that it wasn't necessary for her dad to provide the support and that it wasn't necessary to try continually to please him.

"So, moving on, who in the room is a perfectionist?

"Perfectionism really is not healthy, quite simply, because, as humans, we are not designed to be perfect. If we were perfect, we would never have anything to learn and life would be pretty boring.

"This is my favourite quote from Michael Jordan:

'I've missed more than 9,000 shots in my career. I've lost almost 300 games. 26 times, I've been trusted to take the game winning shot and missed. I've failed over and over and over again in my life. And that is why I succeed.'

"Here are some of Michael's achievements:
- NBA 50th Anniversary All-Time Team.
- Member of six NBA championship teams.
- Five-time NBA Most Valuable Player.
- Six-time NBA Finals Most Valuable Player.
- Ten-time All-NBA First Team.
- Two Olympic gold medals.

"So if it is good enough for Michael Jordan to fail sometimes, why isn't it OK for you?

"OK, here is the next great bit of advice I received: *Ask for help from those who walk the talk!*

"People-pleasers are notorious for not asking for help, which, at best, means that things take a lot longer and, at worse, can lead to a feeling of being totally overwhelmed.

"If you are not good with money …

"Speak to someone who is. What is it that they do, that you don't?

"Find out exactly what it is, right down to the fine detail. Ask not only what they do, but why they do it and what does it bring to them at an emotional and identity level.

"Here are some questions that will help:

- What is it that makes you good with money?
- What goals do you have?
- Why do you have those goals?
- Why are are those goals important?
- And what does that bring you?
- What hasn't worked for you?
- What advice would you give to someone who wants to have more control over their finances?

"If you look at this from a different angle, what you are actually saying is 'Hey, can you share with me the reasons why you are so successful in this particular part of your life?' Who wouldn't want to respond to a question like that?

"It is important to let go of your own reality during these interviews and to keep an open mind. If possible, record the conversation so that you can listen to it over again. My guess is that you will pick up on something that you didn't grasp first time around.

"Once you know their strategies, use the ones with which you feel comfortable. The next step is to:

"Be Grateful!

"Tony Robbins states that:

'When you are grateful, fear disappears and abundance appears.'

"Think of everything for which you are grateful and write them down. Nothing is too small or too basic or too trivial to go on this list. Once you have completed the list, take it with you everywhere and read it out (aloud if circumstances allow) as many times a day as you can.

"The result of reading out your list is totally empowering. How many times a day will you look at yours?

"Again, you can always record the things for which you are grateful, and play back the recording whenever you get the chance. I often play back my affirmations and gratitude lists in the car which often results in puzzled looks when someone else gets in and the playback is still running.

"Brian Tracy says:

'Develop an attitude of gratitude, and give thanks for everything that happens to you, knowing that every step forward is a step toward achieving something bigger and better than where you are now.'

"Next, focus on what you want, not what you don't want.

"Remember, we are looking for the positives to outweigh the negatives. Therefore you have to concentrate on what you want, not what you are trying to get away from. Let the Law of Attraction work for you, not against you.

"A close relative of mine reckons that she is unlucky despite a huge amount of evidence that contradicts this belief. She however concentrates on this belief and guess what? She becomes more unlucky.

"In conclusion, we don't have to remove all the negative beliefs to make progress. If fifty-one per cent of our thoughts are positive, that is enough to make a significant difference. When you reach that tipping point, things will really start to fly.

"All of what I have shared with you today will have been wasted if you ignore the tip I am going to leave you with, and that is to ...

"Take action!

"You can have all the knowledge in the world about a subject, but unless you take action, all of that knowledge isn't worth anything. How many people do you know that don't appear to be as intelligent as you, but are more successful? This is because they take action and make the most of what they have.

"The flipside is that there are many really intelligent people that aren't in the financial position that you would expect them to be in.

"There is a saying that 'knowledge is power'. As Anthony Robbins puts it: *'This isn't true. Knowledge plus massive action equals power.'*

"I could teach you everything you need to know about saving and investing but if you don't actually invest in anything, then you might as well not have learned it in the first place.

"So, to summarise, only you know where you are right now and what you need to do. I hope that, wherever you are on your own particular journey, you now have the clarity of thought to know where that path leads and what you need to do to ensure that you stay on the right path.

"Remember, it is all about the journey and not the destination. Stop every now and again and look back to see how far you have come and make sure you congratulate yourself on your achievements.

"Before we go, we have one last exercise and I like to think I have saved the best for last:

"Close your eyes and picture yourself in the future being who you want to be in life. And ask the following questions:

- What do you look like?
- What are you doing?
- What else do you see around you?
- Who else is with you?

"When that picture is clear, step into that picture and introduce yourself to your future self and ask him or her what it is that you need to do in order to be him or her. At this stage, just trust this process and see what response you get. You may just be surprised."

Alex closed his eyes and decided to ask his subconscious for help. He was pleasantly surprised when he felt a twinge in his stomach and, slowly, he was able to visualise his future self. The picture was of him on stage at Madison Square Gardens, addressing a conference. He was slimmer, looked younger and to the side of the stage he saw a fantastic lady with three children, looking very pleased with him.

Alex stepped into the picture, introduced himself and asked his future self what it was he needed to do in order to become the person who stood before him. The response he received was succinct:

"Find your authentic you, and learn to love that person."

Was that it? Wasn't there a long list of things that he needed to do? His future self spoke again:

"When the pupil is ready the teacher will come."

As Alex tried to make sense of this comment, Jakap spoke again.

"Now, I want you to step into your future self, just for a few moments, to see how it feels."

Nothing ventured nothing gained, thought Alex as he stepped into the vision of his future self. As he did, something amazing happened. He felt like he was almost floating, like a weight had been taken off of his shoulders and he somehow felt taller. He had found the place he wanted to be.

"That exercise is pretty mind blowing," continued Jakap, "and it proves one thing, you have the answers within."

"It has been a pleasure to share some ideas, techniques and my beliefs with you and I hope that whatever the path you take, we remain in contact. There is no greater feeling than when I hear how people have turned their lives around and have improved not only their net worth, but more importantly their self-worth.

"I want to leave you with this last quote from George Monbiot which I have paraphrased:

'Those who are impressed by money are not worth impressing.'

After the usual post-workshop photographs, exchange of phone numbers and the promises to be in touch, Alex started to walk back to his room, feeling strangely disappointed that it had all come to an end. He had learned so much about himself, but there was so much more work to do, and it wouldn't be in the wonderful environment that Jakap had created.

His thoughts were interrupted by someone calling his name; it was Jakap.

"Hi Alex, I was just wondering whether you were staying around for a few days."

"I had planned to go to Vegas for a couple of days, as a base to see the Grand Canyon, not to gamble of course as that would hardly be financial healing."

"I was wondering whether you would like to spend a couple of days with me, some one-to-one work."

"Yes, sure, thank you, but why me?"

"All will be revealed in good time, here is my address, shall we say ten tomorrow?"

"Great, thanks, see you then."

Alex didn't get much sleep that night. His head was full of everything he had learned, trying to piece together the steps he now had to take, what his "future" self had meant about finding his authentic self, and, above all, why Jakap wanted to work with him.

The Grand Canyon would have to wait until he was financially healed.

Final Day Afternoon – Lessons Learned

- Take responsibility for your actions. The day you decide to do it could be one of the most empowering days of your life.
- Complaining is just a waste of time. I have complained a lot in the past. What good has it done me?
- I am no longer the victim. People who play the victim card sap my energy.
- Stop being a people-pleaser. This will benefit not only me, but also those around me.
- Ask for help from those who walk the talk.
- Be grateful for what you already have in this world, many haven't got anything like as much. Develop a mindset of gratitude and the world looks a wonderful place.
- Focus on what you want, not what you don't want.
- Take action! Take action! Take action! Knowledge plus massive action equals power.

Mark Bristow

10 SEARCH FOR THE HERO INSIDE

As the taxi pulled up to Jakap's house, Alex double-checked the address. While the house looked as if it was well maintained and was located in one of the better neighbourhoods, it was definitely not the Hollywood-type mansion that he was expecting. After all, Jakap made a living showing people how to be financially free. This deflated feeling soon disappeared and was replaced by excitement at the prospect of what he would learn over the next two days. He likened this feeling to the way he felt on the day he attended his very first rock concert.

Jakap answered the door. He was dressed very casually in t-shirt and shorts and gave Alex the biggest hug he had probably ever experienced. Alex chuckled to himself and thought about his own very English attitude to greeting people, how his parents were not "touchy feely" people and how he could never imagine his father even hugging another man. His ex-wife had always complained about his reticence to hug and although he agreed to a degree, she probably was not the best teacher as she always hugged members of her family at get-togethers and then promptly complained about them as soon as they were out of earshot. Today, however, hugging felt good.

"Let me take you on a quick tour of the place."

"Yes please" Alex replied, intrigued to see the home of the Financial Healer. Although the house was not as big as he had imagined, it had what some would describe as a nice lived-in feeling about it and seemed to exude positive energy.

With the tour of the house complete, Jakap took Alex through the garden and into the summer house which was divided into two sections. The first section looked pretty much like every other home office with a desk and a laptop and a small filing cabinet. Alex, however, was drawn to an extremely large bookshelf, full of books on self-development, finance, making money and marketing, as well as a section devoted to biographies.

"Have you read all of these?"

"No, not all of them, some of them are more 'shelf' development than self-development," Jakap joked, "but I will get round to reading them all. Reading is one of my greatest pleasures, so much better than having the TV drip-feeding negatives into your soul.

"It wasn't always like that. For a number of years I would be so stressed when I returned home from my nine-to-five, or should that be renamed seven-to-seven, that all I wanted to do was have a TV-dinner and watch any old mindless garbage."

"I think you are describing my life right now," said Alex.

"And that, my friend, is why you are here."

"Yes, I have been meaning to ask you about that. Why did you choose me to come here today?" Alex inquired.

"Well, Alex, there is a very good reason why I have asked you, and that will become clear soon enough. What I can say now is that of everyone at the workshop, you were the one that seemed the most hurt."

"The most hurt?"

"Yes, let me explain. Many people come on this course believing that it will be the answer to all of their problems, and in a way it is. At the very least, it should point you in the right direction. However, after running the workshop for over fifteen years, I can recognise the ones who will put in the work and those who will put the folder on the shelf and come back to it, and they will always come back to it. As the Buddhists say, 'When the pupil is ready, the teacher will appear.'"

"Yes, I keep getting told that."

"You were different, the pain of frustration etched on your face at times made me realise that your time is now. You are ready for what I am about to teach you over the next few days. Shall we do it?"

"Let's go for it," Alex said enthusiastically.

"Good, first off, I want you to list the last three major purchases that you made. When I say major, I mean costing over $500."

"OK, number one, I bought a tailor-made suit that cost $1,500. Let's think, then it was the latest Mac for $2,500 and, finally, I purchased a Bose sound system for $750."

"Could you have found cheaper versions of these items?"

"Well certainly, I didn't have to have the suit tailor-made, that would have saved me $1,000. I guess I didn't have to buy the top of the range computer and if I had bought a cheaper sound system, I doubt I would have noticed the sound difference."

"Great answers, Alex. Now on to the next question, could you have done without the purchases?"

"Well, I guess I could have made do with the suits that I currently own. I didn't desperately need to buy the Mac. I think I could have got another year out of the old one. The sound system, I certainly could do without."

"Hey Alex, this is fantastic. I appreciate your honesty. So, to summarise: you stated you could have bought cheaper versions of these items and, when pushed further, you admitted you could have done without them altogether. Had you not bought the items you would have saved yourself about $4,750 or, put another way, one tenth of your overall debt.

"So, the obvious question is why did you buy them?" Jakap said searchingly.

"Well, the suit was purchased for a wedding and I really wanted to look the part."

"OK, why is that important?"

"To look the part? Well I wanted to give the impression that I was successful."

"And why is it important to give the impression of being successful?"

"Well I want people to think highly of me."

"And why is it important for people to think well of you?"

"So they would like me. When I put it like that it all seems a bit shallow really, doesn't it?"

"Just hold that thought for a moment, let's move on to the purchase of the Mac, why did you buy it?"

"Same reasons really. I wanted to give people the impression that I could afford something new, even if I couldn't. I guess I was thinking that if they knew the level of debt that I had, they would think less of me."

"And the sound system?"

"When I was younger, I was involved with hospital radio for children. In the studio, we had these Bose speakers and Dave, the guy who fitted them, said they were the best speakers available. He would know because he was a sound engineer for the BBC. I made a promise to myself that when I got successful I would buy my own Bose speakers. I guess I just got tired of waiting.

"I told so many people that I would buy those speakers that in the end it was getting so embarrassing I just bought them anyway. That was just a lie; I am still not successful enough to buy them."

"OK Alex, don't go beating yourself up there, this is actually great stuff you are sharing. Do you see the pattern that developed? On each occasion you purchased these items, you were ultimately trying to make people think better of you. Even the sound system which you had previously promised to yourself when you were successful, you eventually purchased so as not to lose face with others."

"So I already knew I do things to please others and now I have discovered that I even buy things because of what others think of me. Does that make me an extra big people-pleaser? I understand that this is not a good trait, but I like helping people," Alex said, confused.

"Helping people is good. It is always better to give than to receive. However, there is a world of difference between helping people and being a people-pleaser. People-pleasers never put themselves first and this is not a good thing. Do you remember when you were on the plane coming over here what the stewardess said to do with the oxygen mask if you have young children with you?"

"The bit that says 'apply the mask to yourself before attending to your children'?"

"Exactly, you can't help others unless you are in a position to do so and that means putting yourself first. I'm going to show you some techniques that will get to the core of why you are a people-pleaser. I think you will be pleasantly surprised at the results.

"In the meantime, I want to introduce some positives to the proceedings. So to start things off, I want you to list three things that you're proud of, these can be anything, absolutely anything."

Alex felt mild panic for a few minutes, had he done anything of which he was really proud? Just as he was feeling that his mind was going completely blank, he recollected a letter his father had written saying how proud he was of him. In the letter, he had given some specific examples and Alex remembered thinking to himself 'yes, I guess these are things to be proud of'.

"OK, the first one has to be completing the London Marathon even though I disliked running."

"Good start, so what was it about completing the London Marathon that made you proud?"

"Well, I ran for a charity so others benefited which was obviously pleasing, but, from a personal point of view, this was something that involved a lot of work and dedication, and I was totally outside my comfort zone. Furthermore, I injured my ankle about three weeks before the marathon and, as a result, I couldn't complete the training programme, yet I still completed the 26.2 miles on the day!"

"That is a fantastic achievement, well done. So what is number two on the list of things of which you are proud?"

"The second one is my work with the hospital radio charity. To be able to help people and to get so much enjoyment, it was just brilliant. You know, I may have had a bad day at work and then I would go into the hospital and there would be children there with cancer and that would put everything into perspective. If I could make a child laugh or smile, it seemed that I had done a little bit to make the world a better place."

"That is just wonderful, and the third thing?" Jakap asked.

"This one has just popped into my head and is a more recent memory. I had a friend who was in pretty dire financial straits and despite my own financial situation I gave her $7,000 on the premise that it was never mentioned again. That became a real eye-opener for me because I realised that I didn't need any recognition for what I had done; just doing it was enough."

"Great job, Alex. Now all we need to do is take the best bits from what you have just told me and cut and paste them into a statement that describes the real you. Based upon what I've written down, I have come up with this:

'An achiever, who helps people without the need for recognition.'

"How does that sound?"

"Pretty good, Jakap, pretty good. Except I don't think I am that person."

"Yet! You are not that person yet, but you know what? From what little I know of you, I reckon that is probably pretty close to the real you and that is the point of this little exercise – to find out who you really are, not who you currently are. We now have an idea of your destination; let's make sure you enjoy the journey. So with this in mind, is this achiever who helps people without the need for recognition doing the right job?" Jakap inquired.

"No of course not, in fact these last few days have highlighted that I need to do something different. I feel like handing in my notice as soon as I get back to England."

"Hang on a minute there! Let's take five before you do anything drastic. You may have realised that there are elements of your job that you dislike at the moment but, to be frank, right now, you need that income. So let's try a bit of reframing here. What are the parts of your job that you like?"

"Well I do get to help people, I guess. I work with a lot of people that I really like and I have worked there for twelve years so it can't be all that bad."

"So, for example, could you stay with your current employer for another year if you knew that, by the end of it, you'd have paid off all your debts and you could go on and do what you really loved?"

"Well, yes, if I knew what it was I wanted to do."

"All in good time, all in good time. So all we have to do now is help you wipe out $50,000 debt, add on a few thousand dollars as your start-up fund and find out what you love enough to want to spend the rest of your life doing. No pressure then," Jakap laughed.

"Well, we're off to a good start. We have identified that your main issue is that you are a people-pleaser and ultimately what you want to be is an achiever who helps people without the need for recognition. Time for some further clarification so that we can plan your journey. Alex, what are your top five values?"

"To be honest, Jakap, I don't think I have ever considered it."

"OK then, in that case, I think the next exercise will be of value. I want you to tell me what is important to you."

"Well, as I think you will have gathered by now, helping others is of great importance; I am also a great believer in fairness and I think that family is of great importance."

"Great, now what does helping others, fairness and family give you?"

"When I help people, I get a sense of well-being; it makes me feel good inside. Fairness just gives everyone the same opportunity and just seems right and family reminds me that I need to look after others rather than just thinking of myself all the time."

"And what else do these things give you, Alex?"

"Do you know what has just come to me? It is a sense of purpose. Helping my family and others is my chance to make the world a better place in my own little way. It is exactly the same as when I visited the children in hospital."

"Hey, great answers, Alex, so what is it you enjoy doing?"

"Well, since about as long as I can remember, I have enjoyed listening to music."

"And what does that bring you?"

"A feel-good factor and sometimes the lyrics of a song can just say how I feel in a way that I never could," Alex said, reflecting on his love of music.

"Anything else?"

"Well, it is on similar lines to what I just said but I am still constantly amazed how a song can change my emotional state in an instant. Also, when I go to see live music, I get overcome by this enormous feeling of well-being, being surrounded by people who are really into whomever we are seeing, just like me."

"Fantastic, a man after my own heart, now to dampen your spirits just a little, what is it that makes you really angry or annoyed?"

"Well, the first one that springs to mind is people not telling the truth, even though I have been guilty of that on many occasions. I also get really annoyed when people take advantage of others; I guess we are back to the fairness thing with that one."

"I guess we are. Tell me, Alex, what is it about these things you have just described that make you so angry or annoyed?"

"Just the total lack of honesty. It always strikes me that if we were all just a little more honest, me included, the world would be a much better place."

"And as an aside, how do you feel when you aren't being honest?"

"I feel lousy."

"That is because you are violating one of your major values."

"Yes, that makes sense now."

"So how about people using others?"

"It is so wrong, why can't we all work with each other and look for that win-win situation?"

"You make a good point there, Alex. So tell me, what would be a better way to deal with these things that make you angry?"

"That is easy: to tell the truth in an elegant way that doesn't offend."

"Well, that seems to be a great way to end part one of the exercise. The next stage is for me to read through my notes and to extract your values."

After a few minutes, Jakap showed Alex the list, "Here, I reckon that this just about covers it." On the list were the words:

- Honesty
- Integrity
- Helpfulness
- Never giving up
- Family

"There are probably many more and I suggest you do more work on this in your own time, but for now, let's rearrange the list in order of how important those qualities are to you. How we achieve this is by comparing each value with the others one at a time. So, I will state the alternatives and I want you to indicate the one that has the greater importance.

"Which is more important, Honesty or Integrity?"

"Honesty," replied Alex.

"Honesty or Helpfulness?"

"Honesty."

"Honesty or Never giving up?"

"Honesty."

"Honesty or Family?"

"Honesty."

"Integrity or Helpfulness?"

"Integrity."

"Integrity or Never giving up?"

"Integrity."

"Integrity or Family?"

"Family."

"Helpfulness or Never giving up?"

"Never giving up."

"Helpfulness or Family?"

"Family."

"Never giving up or Family?"

"Family."

"All we need to do now is add up the totals for each value. The one with the most votes will represent your number one value. Your second highest value has the second most votes, and so on."

Jakap added up the scores. "So, here they are in order:" Jakap said, placing the list in front of Alex:

1. Honesty
2. Family
3. Integrity
4. Never giving up
5. Helpfulness

Alex stared at the answers. "That is amazing, I never would have come up with my values in that order. I would have been sure that Helpfulness would be number one yet it is five. I am shocked that Honesty is number one, given what I have said about not being honest myself and living a lie."

"This is where part three comes in. You now need to give yourself a rating of how you are currently doing for each value. You mark each one out of ten, don't overthink this, just say the first number that comes into your head.

"So for Honesty, out of ten, what number would you give yourself?"

"Four."

"And for Family?

"Eight."

"Integrity?"

"Six."

"Never giving up?"

"Six."

"Helpfulness?"

"Nine."

"Interesting, your highest value has your lowest personal score. Well, we know where you need to concentrate your efforts," said Jakap, encouragingly.

"Yes, I lie to cover up and I hate myself for it. Time to be more honest with everyone and, most importantly, myself."

"It's good to remember that everything we do, we do with a positive intention, based upon our own map of the world. We know now that lying to cover our embarrassment actually hits us at a core value level, which is more hurtful. Remember the 'hall of mirrors' exercise we went through in the workshop?"

"You mean the exercise where I realised I am far too hard on myself."

"Yes, that is the one but, before we start to work on that problem, let's look at what we have achieved so far. We have established your issue and what you would like your outcome to be. We also established your top five values and the areas where more work is required. We are making progress, my friend."

"And we haven't mentioned money once today!" Alex joked.

"Hopefully, you have realised by now that it isn't just beliefs about money and wealth that need to change. In order to make real change, you need to remove some negative core beliefs so that any new beliefs that you form regarding money and wealth are congruent with the authentic you.

"It is my belief that we were not put on this planet to have our lives dictated by limiting negative beliefs and to be preoccupied with trying to live up to other people's expectations of who they think we should be. We should set our goals and dreams by what we deem to be important, not by other people's perceptions. When you are living the authentic you, you will feel comfortable in your own skin, be your own best friend and know your purpose in life.

"Your newly created beliefs should be congruent with the

authentic you and your values. For some, this may mean accumulating as much net worth as possible and that is fine as long as it is done in an ethical way. If you have a lot of money, you can help an awful lot of people. I heard you talking to Martin about J. K. Rowling famously dropping out of the Forbes list of billionaires because she had given away so much to charity. Just imagine what it would be like to be in a position to do such a thing.

"Whatever you want to achieve, it should be in line with who you really are. I love the quote from Wayne Dyer when he says:

'When I chased after money, I never had enough. When I got my life purpose and focused on giving of myself and everything that arrived into my life, then I was prosperous.'

"So let's grab lunch and this afternoon we will change your self-worth."

11 BORN OF FRUSTRATION

As Alex sat out in the sunshine enjoying the breath-taking view of the Californian coastline, he realised that this was a metaphor for how he felt at the moment. He compared it to those numerous rainy days when he was in traffic, travelling to and from a job he did not like, where he worked long hours and was under appreciated. Things were going to get even better.

"This afternoon, I am going to teach you an amazing healing technique that is so easy to learn, you will wonder why the whole world doesn't know of its existence. It is called Emotional Freedom Technique or EFT for short. Most of my clients, when I first teach them, call it that 'tapping thing'."

"Sorry Jakap, I'm still none the wiser."

"Well, you have heard of acupuncture and, I guess that in its very basic form, EFT is pretty much the same except that instead of using needles, we use our fingers."

"Obviously, I have heard of acupuncture but to be perfectly honest I don't really know how it works," Alex admitted.

"Well, Alex, it is like this. The human body is made up of compact energy. The cause of all negative emotion is a disruption in the body's energy system. Acupuncture rebalances the energy system and EFT does exactly the same job.

"EFT is fantastic. It has helped in so many areas that its creator, Gary Craig, says you should try it on everything from feelings of guilt right up to chronic pain and beyond," Jakap enthused.

"And you can get rid of all this just by tapping on yourself?"

"Yes, but rather than spend the next couple of hours talking, trying to convince you of its powers, let's try it out."

"OK, I am certainly willing to try."

"Great, let's start with something basic. Tell me something that is a minor irritant to you."

"OK, this is a really silly one. The sound of wine being poured into a glass somehow irritates me."

"Right, focus on that for a while. When you hear wine being poured, how irritable does it make you feel? Give this a score out of ten, with ten being the most irritable you have ever been, and zero being not irritable at all."

"I guess it is about a seven," Alex estimated.

"Great. You need to trust me on this, we now create a phrase that sets up the negative emotion, so that we can knock it down, Gary Craig describes it as like going bowling. In this case, we are setting up your energy system as though it is the set of bowling pins that we knock down. Let's start with the phrase 'even though the sound of wine being poured into a glass irritates me, I completely love and accept myself'.

"Now, it doesn't actually matter whether you believe that or not at this stage, you just need to say it and after you have been doing this for a while it will seep naturally into your subconscious."

Jakap then explained the rest of the procedure which involved saying the set-up phrase three times before using an abbreviated version whilst tapping on various pre-determined parts of the body.

Initially, Alex felt self-conscious saying out loud that he loved and accepted himself. However, he realised that he would indeed have to love and accept himself before he could help others. After tapping on the various points twice, something strange happened. Alex realised that, whereas before the tapping, his level of irritant was seven out of ten, it had now reduced to four. Three rounds later and the irritant level was at zero.

"Pretty weird first time you do it, isn't it?" interjected Jakap. "But, you know what? Here is the deal, just by tapping, two or three times a day, you can find yourself in a much better place within a matter of weeks. But it can do so much more than just that."

Jakap went on to explain that, in order for EFT to be really beneficial, you have to be more specific. This meant that for every negative emotion that Alex felt, he would have to describe how the emotion felt within his body.

Jakap worked with Alex for the rest of the afternoon, exploring his negative emotions. Alex was constantly amazed how, by merely tapping on certain points of his body, he could reduce and, in most cases, wipe out any negative feelings.

In order to bring the negative emotions to the forefront, Alex would recall a recent memory and describe the negative emotion associated with it. He would then tap on that emotion and after just a few rounds, the intensity of the emotion would reduce, and eventually disappear completely. When Alex then looked back at the memory, the picture looked the same but there was no emotional attachment. "Pretty amazing stuff," he thought.

What is more, it was fun! After the initial reticence about describing his inner feelings (he hardly noticed that he had that many before), he actually enjoyed his set-up statements which increasingly used metaphors, the more often he tried it. Statements like: "Even though I have this grey basketball of frustration in my stomach I completely love and accept myself."

After a couple of hours, it was time to stop.

"How do you feel?" Jakap asked.

"Pretty tired, and I don't think I have drunk so much water in all my life."

"Well you, my friend, have been through an emotional detox so it is hardly surprising."

"I also feel a lot lighter, as if some weight has been taken from my shoulders."

"That is great news but I think that that is enough for one day. But don't worry, there will be even more detoxing tomorrow."

"Jakap, I cannot begin to thank you for all that you are doing for me, but there is one thing that is still troubling me, why pick me for this one-to-one work?"

"All in good time, my friend, all in good time."

12 FATHER TO SON

Alex woke up early the next day after the most relaxing night's sleep he had experienced in as long as he could remember. He had just about managed to stay awake long enough to order a sandwich from room service and finish it before drifting off into a very deep sleep.

Jakap had suggested to Alex that they met at a local school, which at first seemed a little surprising. But when Alex recalled how he had spent much of the previous day tapping on various parts of his body whilst saying out loud that he loved himself, well maybe nothing was going to be that surprising.

Jakap was waiting in the reception area.

"Good morning my friend. I trust you slept well. Welcome to the first school I ever attended. Over there is the room I frequented as a five-year-old, and that is where the lesson begins, because, today, we are going to learn about Matrix Reimprinting."

"Matrix Reimprinting? Is Keanu Reeves going to be joining us then?" Alex quipped.

"Not quite, but I am sure you will find this even more exciting than any film. Matrix Reimprinting is an extension of EFT but with a difference. First, I want to ask what do you think is the fundamental message of the Financial Healer workshop?"

"The message I took away is that our actions are governed by our beliefs, be they good or bad, and our beliefs are created at a time when our conscious mind hasn't fully developed."

"Exactly, remember the story I told about being lost in a department store when I was four. Because my conscious mind hadn't developed sufficiently, I perceived this event to be a major trauma and created a belief that I wasn't loved.

"Let me tell you about my first client which seems appropriate when I tell you her story. Her name is Elizabeth and she came to me, not because of money issues but because she couldn't ever get the body shape she wanted despite endless gym sessions and running a number of marathons. Elizabeth felt that her problem lay in a lack of self-esteem and never being good enough for her parents.

"In order to use Matrix Reimprinting, we try to find the relevant memories that created this belief. Elizabeth had one immediate memory that we worked on. She could remember walking home from school and meeting her mother halfway as usual. Elizabeth had taken a test at school and had come fifth out of a class of forty. She was pleased with the result. We took her back into the memory and I got her to describe what she could see and hear. She could see and hear her mother and herself having a conversation.

"The conversation between Elizabeth and her mother went something like this:

Elizabeth: I had a test today, guess where I came in the class?
Mom: Third?
Elizabeth: No.
Mom: Second?
Elizabeth: Not first.
Mom: Then I don't want to know.

"I then asked Elizabeth to step into the picture and introduce herself to her younger self and ask her how she was feeling. The younger Elizabeth said she was feeling sad because she didn't think that Mom cared. I then asked Elizabeth to talk to her mother and, between them, they spoke to 'young' Elizabeth and explained that Mom was just having a bad day and that she really loved her. They then asked her what she would like to do and she said that she wanted to play in the park so they took her there and I got Elizabeth to capture that image. When I asked her to recall that picture, all Elizabeth could see was her younger version playing in the park.

"You see, Alex, where we have previously believed that all memories are held in the brain and emotions held in our bodies, they are actually held outside. Each cell in our body has receivers that are able to pick up these beliefs and memories, a bit like a TV receiver or a computer that accesses information held in the World Wide Web.

"This area where the memories are held has been called the Matrix or the Morphic field. It is the memories that create or reinforce the beliefs. We can change the memories and, ultimately, the beliefs associated with them, just like changing a TV channel or going to a different website," Jakap explained.

"Very interesting, if a little left field for a financial advisor. Yesterday, when you taught me EFT, we kept going back to memories and working with them. So what is the difference between that and Matrix Reimprinting?"

"Great question, Alex. What happens with EFT is that we tune into memories and re-experience what happened on that day. In doing so, we bring the emotions and feelings created by that information back into the body and we tap on ourselves to actually clear that information. With Matrix Reimprinting, we look at the memory as if we were watching it on a screen so you would see a younger version of yourself in the picture and it is this younger you that is holding on to the trauma. You will then step into the picture to offer advice and help the younger you. By remaining outside of the body, it makes it a lot gentler so the depth of information is incredible; you really get to see the beliefs and patterns, how these events are connected to other events and how the beliefs shape your life and everything you do: your friendships, your relationships, your health. Just about every aspect of your life is down to these early belief systems that all go back to before you were six."

"So, let's get this straight, we look at a 'scene' in the film of my life, I step into the film and change the scene and, in doing so, change the belief I have previously created or reinforced."

"Yes, Alex, that is pretty much it."

"OK, got that, so what you are saying is it's not so much around the trauma of these events, whether it is a huge trauma or a small trauma, it's all about what belief or decision we make at that point, especially when that decision is made pre six."

"Yes it is," Jakap confirmed.

"And it is always pre six because our conscious minds aren't developed at that time?"

"Exactly, in those early years, children are effectively walking around in a hypnotic state. So whatever happens, the beliefs go straight into the subconscious and when it's around a traumatic event, it becomes entrenched. So in my case, the day I got lost in the department store, I made the decision that I was unlovable or my parents didn't love me. Once that belief was in place, I spent my life attracting similar events to validate that belief, something that I was incredibly good at doing. Unfortunately, a lot of what we do is on a negative basis.

"I was told that I was a good child, that I was great even, but the good bits don't go into the subconscious as easily, as there wasn't a lesson to learn. It was good to hear but it wasn't associated with a trauma. When it is associated with a trauma, it gives you a lesson to learn in order that we can survive next time. So sometimes the negative part of childhood does go in to the subconscious and also becomes part of our evolution."

"OK, I think that makes sense, but there is one part of this with which I have a problem and it is this: isn't changing the memory lying? I mean it actually happened and now we are saying that it didn't."

"Another great question. My take is that it isn't lying; the memory is just your perception of an event. Have you ever been to a sporting event where something happened on the field of play and you have a completely different understanding of what has just occurred to the guy sitting next to you?"

"Yes, sure, that has happened."

"This is because you have applied different filters to the memory. At any given time, you will have thousands of bits of information to process. It is not possible to process all this information and, in fact, humans can only deal with seven things (give or take two) at any one time. Therefore, your brain will use filters to deal with this information."

"OK, so what are these filters?"

"They are Deletions, Distortions and Generalisations. Let's consider them in turn.

"Firstly, Deletions are made in a number of ways leading to part of a message being conveyed in an often vague way, so, for example, 'they don't listen to me' doesn't actually tell you who 'they' are or what they don't listen to.

"Distortions can be particularly relevant to anyone in a long-term relationship. My clients often use another expression, 'mind reading', ha ha. Therefore, 'you're not listening to me', 'you never say what you think' and 'you've never liked my mother' are prime examples. Distorted statements can contain an element of assumption. 'You never say what you think therefore you are not interested.'

"Finally, we have Generalisations. If you want great examples of Generalisations, the easiest place to find them is in a newspaper. There, you will see statements like 'experts say' or 'sources close to ...' So who exactly are these 'experts' or 'sources'? Try this for a

Generalisation:

"'I am never good with money' What? Never?"

"I see we are back to our limiting beliefs about money," Alex interjected.

"Exactly, most limiting beliefs have an element of generalisation. By the way, did you notice the generalisation in that statement?"

"I most certainly did!" Alex laughed.

"Our memories are just our perception at the time. I have travelled to places I have visited previously, only to note that they look nothing like how I remembered. This isn't all down to old age."

"I think I understand where you are coming from with this. I have often watched a movie for a second time and certain scenes seem different to how I recalled them first time round."

"In the Matrix, we are not changing the trauma, just how we view it. If you like, we are looking at the event through older, more experienced eyes and putting a whole new perspective on it."

"So we don't rewrite the trauma as such, just how we view it."

"Correct, everyone has been traumatised in their childhood to a greater or lesser extent; all it takes is for a parent to say 'go away I've not got time for you right now' or 'you stupid child, you should be able to do that'. These things will stick and once it sticks, that's it. This explains why you can have children in the same family, with the same parents, attending the same schools and each one will have very different issues based on what has stuck. What initially is seen as possibly a small event creates the negative beliefs that hold you back," Jakap explained.

"And that the older you are, the more evidence you have accumulated, the stronger the negative belief?"

"Absolutely, until you say 'enough is enough' and take action. My ultimate dream would be to see EFT being taught in schools. They're such simple skills but are absolutely life-changing. The average age of people coming to my workshops is forty-three which means they have lived a dysfunctional life for quite a while. If we learn these techniques early in life, there is less negative evidence to clear so change can occur much quicker. Once we release these negative beliefs, we can start creating a fantastic life and a wonderful world."

"And you think that this Matrix Reimprinting is the best way to change these beliefs and create this wonderful world?"

"If they are buried deep in your subconscious, then yes, I do."

"Let's get to work then."

There were plenty of memories to work with:

- The day (aged 2) his sister was born.
- The first day at a new school where he got told off by a teacher for unknowingly going out of bounds (aged 7).
- When he achieved the best results in an exam (aged 10) and was told by the teacher that he was being arrogant, he wasn't.
- The time he was told by his music teacher that he was a lousy singer (aged 15).

On a conscious level, he did not feel as though the memories had left a particularly lasting emotional scar, in fact until he started tapping, he had no recollection at all of his sister being born. But, as Alex was now learning, these memories had been buried deep in his subconscious and had helped create a negative belief that he wasn't good enough.

From what he had learned over the previous four days, this all made sense. However, there was something else, he felt, that was completely inexplicable.

"I don't understand what is going on, Jakap, through all of this I keep experiencing an overwhelming feeling of loneliness. I am not sure where it originates but feel it has something to do with Dad but I am not sure why. He never made me feel lonely and I have never been without friends or family around me."

"Was your dad lonely?"

"I am not sure. He didn't have a wide circle of friends and was an only child but I never thought of him as being lonely. Then again, he wasn't a great one for expressing his emotions."

"OK, Alex, here is the deal, as well as taking on physical traits from our parents and their beliefs, whether intentional or not, it is possible to take on their energy. You could be carrying around his energy and his feelings of being lonely."

"Well, as weird as that may sound, Jakap, you may well be on to something. From what I can gather, he didn't see much of his own dad. He worked away, fought in the war and died at an early age. Could that have something to do with it?"

"You bet it could."

"Back to work then."

They worked long into the night. When they finally finished, Alex began to laugh.

"What is so funny?" Jakap enquired.

"When Harry came to see you, everyone in the office thought that you had brainwashed him. I just thought if they could have seen what we have done today, they would now be convinced. But, as you know, this stuff works; I am honestly starting to believe that I actually deserve to be successful and I know where to go to change my remaining negative beliefs. I would have spent the rest of my life trying to figure this out on a conscious level and never got anywhere. A few days with you and everything seems to fit into place."

"You are certainly making progress but you are not quite there yet," Jakap laughed. "You have been holding on to those negative beliefs for a long time so it may take a little while longer yet. Tomorrow, we go again and it is going to get even better."

Mark Bristow

13 THE FUTURE'S SO BRIGHT I GOTTA WEAR SHADES

Despite working long into the night, Alex woke early, feeling more refreshed and excited than he could ever remember.

There was plenty to be excited about. He felt he had clarity and knew what was required in order for him to be the person he wanted to be. It seemed like an old cliché but he felt like a prisoner who had been shackled by his beliefs for years and now had finally been set free.

The excitement was offset with a hint of sadness because he knew that this was the last day he would be spending with Jakap. He had learned so much from him and being around his positive energy was an absolute joy. However, any feelings of sadness would have to be put to the back of his mind if he were to make the most of what time he had.

They had arranged that Jakap would collect him and for Alex to bring all of his luggage so he could be taken to the airport at the end of the day in plenty of time for him to catch his flight back to the UK. As his flight wasn't until late in the evening, he was slightly surprised as they approached the airport.

"Jakap, you do know that my flight is at 10.00pm not 10.00am?"

"Yes, my friend, but today you are going to be doing a bit more flying than expected. Have you heard of San Luis Obispo County?"

"No, can't say that I have."

"You are going to really love it; the scenery there is fantastic. But that isn't our destination."

"It isn't?"

"No, I have one more place to show you and one more lesson for you to learn."

"I can't wait."

With the flight to San Luis complete, they then picked up their hire car for the final part of the journey. On the way, Jakap asked Alex to recall the scene where he had visualised his future self.

"I can picture myself at Madison Square Garden addressing a huge crowd, telling them how they can change their lives. I look a lot slimmer, younger even, and have a permanent smile on my face."

"Great, what or who else can you see?"

"In the wings, there is a very happy lady with three young children who all seem very proud of what I am doing. They are his wife and children and the future me keeps glancing over to them, he seems very proud."

"It sounds great. What I want you to do now is to step into the picture and introduce yourself to your future self. I then want you to ask him what you need to do in order to get to where he is. Don't think about the answer, just listen to what he says."

"He is saying 'Do the work on yourself, make yourself the best you that you can be, then you will be in the best place to help others.

Take one step at a time, enjoy the journey but, above all else, believe in you.'"

"And how do you feel about that?"

"Fantastic, it all seems great. It is exactly where I want to be."

"Excellent, now before we leave this scene, I want you to step into the body of the future you and tell me what it feels like?"

"Brilliant, just brilliant. I have so much energy and my stress levels are at a minimum. Even better than when I did this exercise before. I am feeling such a warm glow throughout. This is definitely somewhere I want to be. Can I stay here, please?"

"Well if you take the advice of your future self, then it won't be long before you will be there permanently. In order to get there you have to put the work in and get out of your familiarity zone at times. Most people call this the comfort zone but I don't. It is only comfortable in the short term, and who wants to be just comfortable anyway? If you are willing to take the step up and try something new then the future is so bright …"

"I gotta wear shades!" Alex joked. "I now realise that I can step up and feel great or take the easy route and stay frustrated. In reality, there is no choice at all. If I stay doing what I have been doing, I am going to end up getting the same results. That is not all: I will have wasted all your generous training and will be letting you down."

"No, Alex, you will be letting yourself down. Remember, if you want to be happy, you have to be the best you that you possibly can be."

"As usual, you are so right!"

"The best way to get good at visualisation is to practise." Jakap had told Alex, so, despite the fantastic scenery, he closed his eyes and visualised everything he wanted in his life.

Jakap had also stressed the importance of visualising removing all the unwanted items that were holding him back.

"How do I do that?"

"OK, think of something that is holding you back in life, stopping you from being where you want to be."

"Well, there is obviously a lack of belief in myself; I have certainly worked that out over the last few days."

"Great, now think of a metaphor that describes this lack of belief."

"It is like a wall around me that I just can't break through; it is like that Pink Floyd video for 'Another Brick in the Wall' where the wall surrounds the guy and there is no way out. Let's call it the 'Pink Floyd Wall'."

"So we have the 'Pink Floyd Lack of Belief Wall'," Jakap suggested.

"That's it, I have spray painted 'lack of belief' all over the wall."

"Fantastic, so how are we going to get rid of this wall?"

"We are going to chip away at it gradually"

"We?" Jakap asked.

"Yes, I can see some people helping me, even though I don't know who most of them are. You are there of course, and I can hear 'A little help from my friends' playing in the background."

"Fantastic. You are right, you may not know some of these friends yet, but you will. When the time is right, they will appear. You must also be prepared to accept that you will lose some of your existing friends along the way, but that is OK. You just have a different agenda to the one that they will continue to follow."

"Yes and I am guessing that some of those will be the energy sappers?"

"Oh yes, and those who have taken advantage of your generous nature in the past. You won't have time for them anymore. Let's fast forward to the time when this 'lack of belief wall' is finally knocked down, what happens then?"

"Well, the shadow created by the wall has disappeared and has been replaced by blue sky and sunlight, lots and lots of bright warm sunlight. I reach for my shades because the future is so bright!"

Alex reached into his bag for his journal and wrote the following:

- The power of visualisation.
- Just bricks in the wall.
- I'll get by with a little help from my friends.
- The future's so bright …

Mark Bristow

14 ALL YOU NEED IS LOVE

Alex sat back, relaxed and enjoyed the beautiful scenery for the rest of the journey. For the first time in a long while, he felt he was living in the moment, a human being, rather than a human doing.

"So where are we going, Jakap?"

"We are going to Hearst Castle, built for the newspaper mogul William Randolph Hearst. It is built on the top of a hill; there are four buildings, 165 rooms, two swimming pools and 250,000 acres. A little cramped but somehow they got by!"

Despite being primed by Jakap, Alex was still taken aback at the enormity of the building and the sheer number of rooms. While he admired the large amount of artwork that would rival most museums, his overriding thought was "just one family lived here".

After the official tour had ended, Jakap ushered Alex outside.

"Just look around. At one time, everything you could see was part of the Hearst estate, pretty impressive, huh?"

"I guess you are saying that you can have anything you want if you dream big enough, that is why you have brought me up here, right?"

"Well, while that is certainly true and is a belief I would endorse, it isn't the reason that I asked you to come here. Here is the story: Hearst spent the last thirty years of his life with an actress and model named Marion Davies. When he died, he left fifty-one per cent of his estate to Marion who promptly sold it back to the Hearst family for one dollar a year plus a bit of publicity for her charity."

"She gave up fifty-one per cent of this?"

"Yes, you can have every material thing you desire, but if you can't share it with those whom you love, it isn't worth a dime. In my experience, given a choice of love or money, there is no contest."

"I guess you don't want to be the richest man in the world if you have no one to share it with," Alex pondered.

"You certainly don't. Come on, it is time to go."

On the journey back, Alex reflected on the story of William Randolph Hearst and Marion Davies. On the radio, Dire Straits were singing about 'Love over Gold' when Jakap spoke, "I think it is time for me to apologise."

"Why? Whatever for?"

"Well, for these last few days, I have avoided answering your question about why I chose to mentor you. The reason I didn't answer was because I wanted to ensure that you received the complete picture and you were the right person for the job."

"Job, what job?"

"Alex, I have been working as the Financial Healer for the last twenty years and loved every minute of it. I am now in the position financially where all the pieces are in place to provide me with the income that my family need for the rest of our lives. Sure, I could carry on working as I am for another few years and move to a bigger and better house but why would I do that? The only reason to do it would be to impress other people and I stopped playing that game a long time ago.

"Life is great and the time is right to take things to the next stage. I want to get my work into schools and colleges so that when kids get out into the real world, their financial decisions are made based on a bedrock of strong positive beliefs rather than negative ones.

"Now there are two certainties around this new project. Firstly, I will have to do a lot of unpaid work to prove it works and secondly, that the 'Financial Healer' name won't cut it with the kids. So I am going to have to dream up something new. In the meantime, I want financial healing to continue. This is where you come in."

"How?"

"I want you to be the new Financial Healer."

"Me, why me?"

"I have been planning this for a little while. I need someone to pick up the baton and from what I have seen, I believe that you are the one. Over the last week, I have seen total frustration turn to extreme positivity. I think I know how badly you want to change. So, are you interested?"

"Interested? You bet!"

"Fantastic, that was the answer I was hoping for. I can now start planning. There is one condition which I have to set though. First of all, you have to 'walk the talk'. You have to get yourself out of debt and prove, once and for all, that you are in control of your financial situation, not the other way around. Once you have done that, well things can move pretty quickly."

The carrot had been dangled, Alex and Jakap spent the rest of the journey planning just how quickly Alex could become the new Financial Healer. He figured if he cut back on unnecessary expenditure, devoted more time to planning and worked on changing his self-worth, he would be ready in a year.

"In that case, you have six months to be ready. If you don't think you can do it in six months, then you aren't thinking big enough."

"OK, six months it is, I will be ready in six months."

"Looking forward to it, my friend, looking forward to it."

15 CELEBRATION DAY

S till with a sense of disbelief, Alex boarded the flight home. A week ago, he had landed at the same airport thinking he was at the last chance saloon. He was leaving with the greatest incentive possible, the opportunity to be the Financial Healer.

There was no time to lose; he had made a commitment to Jakap. He would be ready in six months. He opened his journal and wrote the heading 'WHY?' He then listed all the reasons why he had to finish the task on time. Two hours later, the page was full. The 'Why' was big enough, now. Next it was time for the 'How?'

On the next page, he created two more headings, 'How I am Going to Save Money' and 'Total Savings over Six Months'. For the next hour, he listed the various ways he was going to save money:

Eliminate take-out coffees	$ 390
Make my own lunch	$ 650
No take-out meals	$ 520
Cancel subscriptions to 'get rich schemes'	$ 3,600
Cancel magazine subscriptions	$ 500
Restrict major socialising (no taxis)	$ 1,350

Stop buying clothes	$ 1,000
No purchase of music	$ 260
No purchase of concert tickets	$ 1,200
Cancel gym membership	$ 1,000
Cancel cable TV	$ 600
Get someone to share the house (rent and bills)	$ 3,000
Sell the car, buy something smaller and cheaper	$ 7,000
Savings on running costs on 'new' car	$ 1,000
Car insurance savings	$ 300
Park further away from the office, avoid parking costs	$ 1,300
Don't renew football season ticket	$ 1,000
Sell unwanted DVDs, CDs, mobile phones	$ 600
Use unused store vouchers	$ 300

As he looked down the list and totalled up the savings, he was pleasantly surprised at the total $25,570, over fifty per cent of his target, a lot higher than he had initially hoped. He studied the list again and realised there were secondary benefits to be had: he would have more time. There was to be no more time wasted watching garbage TV or going out, getting drunk and spending the next day nursing a hangover.

Time would be saved as there would be no more searching on the Internet for the next "get rich" scheme. From now on, his reading would be focused on books and articles that were in alignment with what he now knew was his life purpose. Jakap had provided him with a list of his favourite authors and he had made a promise that his spare time would be used to invest in himself.

Alex had now been given the opportunity to change people's lives and he was not going to give it up.

There was still the small question of the remaining $25,000 that was required to pay off the debts but Alex was confident that he was capable of achieving this goal. No longer was his time going to be cheap. No longer would he give discounts to clients.

On reflection, he had realised he had such a low opinion of himself that he was always offering discounts, sometimes when they hadn't even been requested. He would also demand a larger percentage of any bonuses earned when working jointly with a colleague.

Jakap had told him that he was probably spending most of his time on the clients that gave him the most hassle. Unless they were a huge source of income, then these clients should be avoided. They were just "energy sappers that take all your positive energy and replace it with their own negative energy".

Alex went through his client list and realised that it was those clients who actually provided minimum income and maximum stress.

Over the next six months, his life changed dramatically. He found a friend, Dave, who was happy to house share as he was separating from his wife, but "on speaking terms". He was tidy around the house, had a hectic social life and was out most of the time, which suited Alex. Although Dave often asked Alex to join him, Alex stuck to his game plan.

Alex didn't miss garbage TV or takeaways. He actually started to enjoy cooking and the removal of processed foods was good for his health. When he did go out, it was to play team sports, which had a social element, was cheap and helped him to lose weight. He was pleased this meant that he no longer had to pay for membership to a gym, which he did not use anyway.

He did not miss going out and getting drunk and certainly did not miss the next-day hangover. Surprisingly, he did not even miss going to concerts or buying new music. Instead, he revisited and rearranged his existing collection and fell in love again with some old songs and sold those that had now been filed into the newly christened "whatever was I thinking of?" section.

There were many advantages to having a smaller, cheaper car, not least it was so much easier to park, and needed much less time to clean.

At work, he found that he actually gained respect from the majority of his colleagues when he asked for a bigger slice of the pie. To those who did not respect him more, he just smiled and left them to it while thinking of the time he would save.

Alex was pleasantly surprised to find that the clients with whom he enjoyed working did not even raise the issue of discounts because they were happy with his work. He sought out the "energy sappers" and suggested alternative ways of dealing with the organisation without his involvement.

Alex focused on the job in hand, working from home as much as possible so as not to get involved in too much office banter. He only checked his emails twice a day (if it is that important, they will ring) and although, initially, he would open his inbox with a certain amount of trepidation, he soon realised he was in fact right. If it was urgent, they did call.

There was one final technique he had learned from Jakap that he put into daily use. Before each task, he asked himself three questions:

- Does this task need to be done?
- Is there anyone else who can do this task?
- Does it need to be done today?

The result of these small but important changes resulted in increased efficiency, giving him more time to take on new clients and he encountered less stress. At the end of the first quarter, his net bonus after tax was $15,095. In the second quarter, the benefits of working smart rather than hard really started to pay dividends and he received a bonus of $23,260, enough to pay off the remainder of his debts, have some funds in reserve and buy a ticket to California.

It was time to make that call.

ACKNOWLEDGMENTS

The Financial Healer wouldn't have ever seen the light of day without the inspiration, support and positive energy from some very special people especially the EFT, Matrix Reimprinting and NLP communities of which I am proud to be a part.

Specifically I would like to thank:

- My clients for providing the inspiration for the book and their constant support. It has been an absolute pleasure to work with you all.

- John Seymour and his team at JSnlp for introducing me to NLP and helping me remove my limiting beliefs that held me back for years.
  http://www.jsnlp.co.uk

- Karl Dawson. One of the most humble and helpful yet extraordinary men I have ever met. Thank you Karl for showing me the beautiful yet simple techniques that are EFT and Matrix Reimprinting, and for your constant help.
  http://www.efttrainingcourses.net

- For a practical demonstration of EFT, go to:
  www.financialhealer.co.uk/my-videos

- Everyone at Peter Thomson International. Without their support and training I would never have even contemplated writing a book.
  http://www.peterthomson.com

- Everyone in the EFT North West group for their feedback on the numerous early drafts and their continual enthusiasm.

- Manoj Vilayan for his brilliant cover design.

- Deborah Hartmann, Hannah Briggs and Rochelle Marsden for their proofreading skills.

- Alun Richards for his feedback and technical know-how.

- The team at Digital Visitor.

- Erik Cornish for coming up with the initial concept of the Financial Healer.

- And finally to my family and friends for their ongoing enthusiasm, support and belief.

Thank you all.

ABOUT THE AUTHOR

Mark Bristow is a financial coach/mentor, broadcaster and author based in south Manchester in the UK. He specialises in helping people remove their mental blocks preventing them from leading the abundant life they deserve. He is a trainer in Emotional Freedom Techniques (EFT), a Neuro Linguistic Programming (NLP) master practitioner and a Matrix Reimprinting practitioner.

Previously, Mark worked in financial services where he held a number of positions in FTSE 100 companies including Pensions Manager at the UK's largest individual financial adviser.

Mark has his own radio show on EFT Radio online and has been interviewed by the BBC and featured in the *Daily Express*.

Mark lives in Bramhall, Cheshire with his wife, three children, one grandchild and numerous pets.

Mark's website is www.financialhealer.co.uk

07778667617.

Printed in Great Britain
by Amazon